Guided

Imagery

for Cancer

Harness the power of your
Mind to heal your Body

By Avinoam Lerner

ISBN-13:978-0692401767

ISBN-10:0692401768

AvinoamLerner.com
Free@AvinoamLerner.com

Exclusive Members Access
Go Here Now
For
More FREE Content

www.AvinoamLerner.com/guided

Guided Imagery is a safe and gentle practice anyone can benefit from. For some it is an intuitive process, for others a skill need be learned.

This exclusive bonus (available only to those who purchased this book) offers further support, insight and guidance to help you get the most of your practice.

May it be of service to you.

With joy,
Avinoam Lerner

Get Immediate Access

www.AvinoamLerner.com/guided

Table of Contents

Legal Disclaimer

While Guided Imagery or any other methods of conditioning i.e. Creative Visualization, Visual Imagery, NeuroLinguistic Programming has many beneficial effects, cannot and will not substitute any current or future professional medical or psychological care or treatment, and if any concerns i.e. medical or psychological arise, you should first consult a qualified health care provider for diagnosis, advice and care.

Guided Imagery or any of the scripts or products offered in this book is not intended to diagnose, treat, cure nor prevent any disease or illness. Never listen to Guided Imagery or self-conditioning recordings while driving a car or operating machinery. It is your sole responsibility to always choose an environment that is quiet and safe.

Avinoam Lerner makes no claims as to how soon results can ensue or their permanency. His scripts, audio recordings, suggestions and instructions are intended for the purpose of self-help and personal use only. Avinoam is a certified hypnotherapist, not a licensed physician or a licensed mental health professional. He does NOT claim to provide any form of health care or psychotherapy and does not represent his services as any form of medical, behavioral or mental health care.

For best practice, please consult your health care provider before making any health care decisions or for guidance about the benefits of Guided Imagery for any specific medical condition.

What is Guided Imagery?

Guided imagery is the process of focusing the mind by engaging the creative faculty we call imagination. It utilizes our ability to create mental visions and images and project them onto the screen of our mind's eye. We are all endued with this ability whether we are aware of it or not… it is as simple as day dreaming or calling forth a memory from long ago.

Using guided imagery we can explore the relationship between that which we hold in our mind and that which we experience in the body and utilize, this mind body connection, for healing and recovery.

You may already have some experience with Guided Imagery or at the very least heard about its many benefits in healthcare. It might be something that you stumbled upon while doing your research online, something a friend or family member mentioned or even something that your doctor recommended as a way to improve the quality of life between visits.

Over the past few decades Guided Imagery has gained a solid reputation and there is a lot of information (as well as misinformation) out there on the topic. This is why it is vital that before you get started with this book suggested scripts, that you'll understand exactly what it is and why it is such a valuable tool in cancer care. If you are not excited yet about the many benefits Guided Imagery offers you certainly will by the end of this booklet; because regardless of your whether or not you believe it will work... it will work! The reason I know that is because you have been practicing Guided Imagery for many years. Yes, you have!

The most common use of Guided Imagery, or should I say misuse of Guided Imagery is... Worry, yes worry... and if you are human you have done much of that already.

Think for a moment about the practice of WORRY. When you worry you engage your imagination in things that have not happened yet. They have not happen and may never happen and still your mind is generating scenarios, most if not all are negative and based in fear. Now, when you worry, do you feel good? Is it pleasant? Of course not, nevertheless you engage in it because you feel threatened and have legitimate concerns.

In this booklet I will show you how to engage the same mental faculties you do when you worry but in a healthy way, a way that will promote a sense of wellbeing and comfort rather than fear and discomfort. All you need is an open mind and the willingness to follow my guidance. If you will, you will certainly benefit from this practice in the same way every other person in my care have.

Guided Imagery is similar in many ways to daydreaming but the difference will be that Guided Imagery is structured and has a specific goal. The Thesaurus of Psychological Index Terms officially defines Guided Imagery as a "mind-body technique involving the deliberate prompting of mental images, used in the treatment of mental disorders, for performance enhancement, and in helping patients cope with diseases and their symptoms" (2001). That may sounds vague but, in practice, it is not so different from the basic act of imagining which we all do every day.

For a few brief moments each day, we all lose ourselves in our thoughts. You might be at work or lying in bed and suddenly find your mind has transported you somewhere else. Suddenly, you are no longer aware of your physical surroundings. Your brain has taken you somewhere far away and you hadn't even realized that it was happening. It can happen when we are worrying about something or looking back on a fond memory.

Like so many other innate tools, we can use our minds and thoughts to create positive experiences or negative ones. We can lift ourselves out of a mundane experience or we can drown ourselves in the concerns of daily life. It is truly but a choice for each and every one of us. It may not always feel this way but it is true, and while it might feel like our circumstances have created our states of mind, in reality, it is the other way around.

Every person has his or her own unique journey in life and we will all face a vast array of challenges, illness and cancer is but one of them. These challenges in and of themselves do not define us. What will define us is how we choose to look at these challenges. While cancer is a major obstacle and undoubtedly has many negative connotations, we can still choose how to view and experience it. We can make the best of it or we can allow it suffocate us. Guided Imagery seeks to teach its practitioners how to release their minds from the grip of stress, anxiety and fear that burden our minds and inhibit the healing capacity of our bodies.

As I have said, you can think of Guided Imagery as similar to daydreaming but there are many important differences. We know how to daydream from childhood but most of us never really learn to harness the spectacular power of our imaginations. Our minds can truly accomplish impressive feats and it is important to learn how to use this incredible instrument.

You wouldn't begin driving a car without reading an instruction booklet first and I believe that we can look at our imaginations in a similar way. Our minds have so many different facets that even hundreds of years of scientific study has not yet given us a complete picture of how it all works. Guided Imagery gives us a small piece of the manual that we need to begin using our brains to their fullest potential.

One thing that makes Guided Imagery distinct from daydreaming is the direction that you receive through the narration. In this Guided Imagery for Cancer program, we aim to teach you where to direct your thoughts and how to use them productively. Now, if you simply tell yourself to just think of something positive, you often get lost in thoughts. This happened to me all the time before I began using Guided Imagery. I would be in a stressful situation and just tell myself to think about something positive. It was a great idea, in theory, but it was never effective for me. It would not last. It was only once I learned how to harness the power of imagery that I could actually stop dwelling on the negative things that were cluttering my mind.

To use imagery productively, you need some guidance. You need to learn how to let go off your negative emotions and focus your brain before you can realize all of the profound effects of Guided Imagery. One of the great things about it is that, after practicing Guided Imagery, you will be able to use it anytime, anywhere and without guidance. You will not need to get into a quiet room or use any other stereotypical aspect of meditation. After some practice, it will simply become second nature to you.

Guided Imagery has been described as "a gentle but powerful technique that focuses and directs the imagination" (Naparstek, 1994). As your guide, my goal is to teach you exactly where and how to direct your imagination. We are all unique and therefore relax in different ways. My goal is to help you find your best way to relax. You don't need to be creative or have a vivid imagination, you simply need to make an effort and have a true desire to allow your mind and body to relax.

"We can change the whole world just by altering the way in which we perceive it. "
Avinoam Lerner

The power of our minds never ceases to amaze me. We can change the whole world just by altering the way in which we perceive it. If you are dreading walking outside on a cold day, you can make yourself shiver just by picturing the icy air hitting your face. On the same chilly day, if you recall the last time that you were lying on the beach relaxing under the sun, you might find yourself warming up and forgetting about the cold for a moment. Our brain is a profoundly potent tool. We can use it to worry about things that may never happen or allow ourselves to be soothed by wonderful experiences that we may never have.

Before you begin practicing the scripts included in this booklet or listening to any audio or even the CDs included in my Guided Imagery for Cancer program, I would like you to try this very quick exercise of your imagination. It will help you experience first-hand the power of your own mind and imagination.

Look at a picture of a lemon, any lemon. It doesn't matter if it's an actual lemon you got you're your kitchen or just a picture you found online or in a cooking book, just spend a moment looking at it and try to notice if it affects you in any way... there may not be much of a reaction and that's ok. If there is simply take a mental note of it and how intense or real it may feel.

Now let's try to do the same thing but this time we're going to involve our imagination. First, read the next few lines so you'll know what you need to do. Then, close your eyes... and imagine that you are holding a ripe and juicy sour lemon in your hand... allow the lemon to become real to you in all of its dimensions and in your mind's eye, see its bright color... smell its citric scent, and even feel its weight in your hand, how heavy with juice this slice is. When you have, imagine that you cut that lemon in half, making sure to not get the juice all over your shirt... and gently bring that half a lemon toward your mouth. As you do that, imagine that you open your mouth wide and squeeze all that sour sour lemon juice right into your mouth... feel the juice pour onto your tongue... feel the lemon juice surround your tongue and begin pooling up inside of your mouth. Give the sour juice a good swish so you can savour the stingy taste and notice what is taking place within and around your mouth.

Done correctly, it is likely that you have felt some kind of tingling sensation in your mouth, perhaps even salivation; this is very normal and even expected. If you have not, do not despair, some people really like lemon juice and therefore the experience is different. Simply try the same exercise but this time with a very sour pickle. Imagine yourself biting into that sour pickle etc.

This imagery exercise demonstrates the power of your imagination. When we just looked at the image of the lemon we only engaged one of our senses (sight), we were not truly involved with what we gazed upon. To fully engage with the lemon we need to utilize multiple senses, sight, taste, smell etc. This is the power of imagery and our imagination.

Think about the difference between chatting with a friend online or by telephone and actually seeing them in person. When we send messages online, we are only using our eyes. You may be able to recall what your friend wrote to you but you won't be able to create the same vivid memories that you can when you actually see a person. It can be a bit more engaging to talk on the phone but it often still feels like something is missing.

When we are physically together with people, all of our senses are engaged in the activity. Even the simple act of sitting at a table with a person whom we see every day engrosses our bodies. You can see the person, feel the chair underneath you, and smell the air around you. Every aspect of the experience will influence how you perceive the interaction. If there is a sweet smell in the air, you might find a dull conversation more enjoyable. If the chair is uncomfortable, you might quickly tire of experience.

It is rare that we realize it on a conscious level but our senses are working together all of the time. Our body is constantly taking in new sensations and sending messages to our brain. This interaction between our mind and body creates a profound impact on the way in which we perceive everything and everyone around us.

When we are talking about Guided Imagery, it is critical to remember the importance of using each one of your senses. Some people consider the idea of things like meditation or Guided Imagery to be dull because they just envision themselves sitting in a room doing nothing. While it may be true that your physical body is doing nothing, your mind is being extremely active. If you think back to the times that you have spent daydreaming, you know that you don't have to physically do anything to feel like you are being active.

Remember back to a time when you were truly excited about something. When we think about something that we are looking forward to, we are fully engaged in our thoughts. There is nothing boring about just sitting still and picturing what it is that we are craving, especially when we envision ourselves thriving with health and vitality. In contrast, when we misuse Imagery as in the case of worry and anxiety they consume us. When we are using our mental capacity to dread something, it can exhaust us.

It is tiring to us not just mentally but also physically. If you are stressed for a long period of time, your body might start to feel like it is barely dragging along.

This relationship between our body and mind is nothing short of spectacular. When we look at our favorite food, we can almost taste it. When we recall a fond embrace, it is as if we can actually feel it. When we smell certain scents, we feel like we have been transported though time.

Do you remember the lemon/pickle exercise and how it made your body react? This is one of the amazing tricks performed by our body that has prompted researchers around the world to really take a close look at Guided Imagery.

When we sense our salivation over the mental imagery of the lemon, we realize that our imagination affects more than our mind, it affect our body. The physiological response shows that we can use mental imagery to create very real responses in our bodies. Having said that, we of course do not need to practice Guided Imagery for our bodies to create the physical response, it does it all by itself. All we are aiming to do is to tap into this remarkable relationship between thoughts, imagination and the physical body to improve our experience and ability to recover.

The best part about this fascinating mental power of imagination is that we can harness this ability to do far more than just make ourselves drool. We can promote certain mental experiences that will lead to true physical changes. It may sounds too good to be true but it is every bit real and imply amazing.

Guided Imagery is based around this simple principle. If we are able to create physical changes with our minds, why not use our minds to make ourselves healthier and happier? We may not be able to fix everything just by thinking blissful thoughts but we can definitely have a positive impact. If you create harmony and happiness within your mind, your body will grow stronger and better be able to face the challenges of life. Let me be very clear, Guided Imagery is not wishful thinking; it has a real scientific foundation that has been established through decades of research.

With practice, all of us can learn to make healthier and more resilient "blue prints" for our brains. We can create memories of times when are bodies and minds are engaged in something that they truly love. It doesn't matter if we look back on positive experiences that we have had or if we just think up some new ideas that make us happy.

Often when we are facing the unknown realm of illness, fear sets in and we activate the fight-or-flight mode that wears our bodies down quickly. When faced with long-term stress, our bodies begin to feel like they are perpetually in this fight-or-flight mode. It impacts us both physically and emotionally. This physical response was lifesaving to our ancestors. It enabled them to react quickly to dangerous situations and was an extremely powerful tool.

In modern life, when we are rarely in a life or death situation, our brain still act by constantly being in the "ON" mode when we encounter stress and this is where our new and improved "blue prints" can come in handy. Once we create our blue prints, we can use them anytime that we need them.

With some guidance and practice, anyone can learn to transition from having basic daydreams into using Guided Imagery productively. You may have heard advice before on the value of recalling positive memories when you are under stress. You often see people with photos on their desks or images on their computers of vacations, family members, or just relaxing scenes. They do this, of course, because it reminds them of happy times in their lives. It is a great way to deal with the stress of work or just relax whenever you need it.

It is not enough, however, to just look at a photograph. If you remember my previous example of the lemon or pickle, you know that a two-dimensional photo is just not enough to really transport a person. To truly change your state of mind, you need to use more than just your eyes. Your entire Self needs to be transported to a different place.

If you have a fond memory of yourself lying on the beach and want to use it as a tool for relaxation, you need to recall all of the sensations associated with it. You need to feel the sun on your skin, smell the scent of salt in the air, and taste a fresh sip of lemonade circling around your tongue. The more present your body is in this memory, the less aware you will be of the present moment and its stressors. In basic terms, this is the foundation of Guided Imagery. It helps you to take your mind to a peaceful place that allows the entirety of your body to relax and feel at ease.

The objective of Guided Imagery is to teach you how to create these positive states of mind and use them productively. Stress is negative to our minds as well as our bodies. By relaxing your mind, you feel better in the short-term while facilitating your body's natural ability to fight illness in the long run. And, of course, even if we can't have healthy bodies at every moment, we can have healthy minds. One of the goals of Guided Imagery is keep your mind at the peak of health.

Like most things in life, Guided Imagery becomes easier with practice. You may be a bit tense and apprehensive the first time you work through a program but each time it will get progressively easier and feel more natural. It is really so simple that you may feel like you are doing something incorrectly. We have been so conditioned to believe that true reward only comes after struggle but that is simply not always the case.

With Guided Imagery, you will find your greatest rewards come after you give up your desire to struggle. When you allow your mind to be at peace, your body will begin to relax and it will radiate through the entirely of your being. All you need to do is follow the simple instructions of the narration and permit your mind to drift away.

When you let go of the tension that you have been carrying, you will find that you feel lighter. A burden will lift from your shoulders. While you can only realize this on a cognitive level, your body will also realize it on a physical level. As you begin to feel more at peace internally, your body will react to and be able to function more productively.

Once you have created your new and improved mental blueprint and have a favorite "place" to go to in your mind, Guided Imagery will become second nature. You will no longer need to sit down at home with your CD or MP3 player. Your mind will be able to recall the path that it took in the past to achieve contentment.

Once your blueprint is readily available to you, you will be able to harness a great level of power. Whenever you are feeling overwhelmed or just down, you can take out your blueprint and allow your worries to drift away. The best thing about this is that you can do it anywhere at any time. There is no preparation to be done and you don't need any special tools. It is a gift that will forever be held within your mind.

Who Can Benefit from Guided Imagery?

Guided Imagery is a great tool for anyone who wishes to take part in their own healing and care. One of the best things about it is that it can be used anywhere at any time. You don't need any special skills and it is not difficult to learn how to do it. Everyone needs a bit of practice to truly use Guided Imagery productively but you will quickly improve your skills with a bit of practice.

While serious conditions merit medical care and the use of medication, Guided Imagery is a wonderful accompaniment to it. It can help to lessen fear and anxiety, reduce severity of side effects, improve sleep and quality of life and so much more.

In cancer care, Guided Imagery can help patients mentally prepare for medical procedures, as well as recover from these procedures more rapidly. It can help strengthen their emotional, spiritual and physical resilience and enhance their resolve to heal.

Guided Imagery can also be great for those who are supporting a friend or family member who has cancer. Even though they are perfectly healthy, it may start to feel like cancer is taking over their lives. It is easy to forget how stressful it is for our loved ones when we are facing a major struggle in our lives. When you are trying your best to support someone important in your life, you are always trying to put your own concerns and needs at bay. Guided Imagery can be a major asset for managing anxiety and depression for those going through cancer care as well as the people in their lives.

Major life changes also cause major changes to our daily routines. We often don't realize how important the mundane parts of everyday life are until we can no longer do them. When we have days where we can't go to work or go for evening walks or whatever other things we used to do every day, it is easy to become disheartened and anxious. When we are ill and spending extra time in bed or at home, feelings of sadness can creep up quickly. It can start to feel like we have too much time alone with our thoughts. We can start to feel sorry for ourselves or feel like we're drowning in our thoughts. If you are feeling a bit of cabin fever or just need to clear your mind, Guided Imagery is a priceless tool. The idea of spending quiet time alone with your thoughts might feel a bit intimidating but it really should not be, especially once you have learned how to use imagery to guide your mind.

Guided Imagery is much more than just an instrument for relaxation. It can help people cope with pain management, overcome nausea, prepare for biopsies and transplants and even spring our immune system into action. Now, rest assures that in order to benefit you don't need to be a creative person or have a strong imagination. You don't need to be a relaxed person or have experience with meditation. The only thing you absolutely need is a bit of dedication. You don't need to go to a retreat or spend hours learning the skills of a monk. You just need to keep your mind open to that which naturally arise within you, and keep practicing it for a bit until something clicks with you. It is not solely a mental exercise so it doesn't matter if your concentration level isn't great or if your attention span is short. You only need to let go of yourself a little and allow your entire body to give into your mind. You need however utilize your emotions and all of your sensations to embrace the experience.

Even if you have tried other relaxation techniques in the past to no avail, Guided Imagery might be right for you. Everything has a time and a place and there is no reason to despair if you have previously tried a relaxation method that didn't work for you. It may not have been the right time in your life to try it or you simply may not have been in the right mood that day. Every relaxation program is different.

Meditation is different from Guided Imagery and, even within the category of Guided Imagery; there are many types and styles. It is simply a matter of finding the program that is right for you. You would never try a potato then say that vegetables aren't for you just because you didn't like that potato ☺. Of course, we know that there are many ways to prepare potatoes and that they certainly don't represent all vegetables. It's therefore important to remember this idea and apply it to other areas of our lives.

The bottom line is that everyone can practice Guided Imagery and benefit from it. Women and children tend to take to it more quickly but nearly anyone can use it productively. Your education level, age, gender, race, and health are irrelevant. It's a nature ability inherit in all of our brains.

A fascinating study was recently done with congenitally blind patients. Researchers found that not only are blind people able to have visual dreams but they are also able to use imagery. The study found that blind patients were using their visual cortex to process the things that they had heard and touched. They used the information from their other senses, such as sounds, textures, and smells, to create a visual image in their mind (Bertolo, 2005).

One of the most interesting aspects of this study is that means that we don't need to every have experienced something to imagine it. Even if we are not creative people or if we don't have any idea what an actual experience would be like, we can image it. We can create images that can trick our brain into momentarily believing that we are actually having these experiences.

The key aspect of Guided Imagery is that it helps your body to relax. Needless to say, this is useful for absolutely everyone, especially while undergoing treatment or while recovering from one. As we so often hear, stress takes a toll on your body. If you can negate the negative effect of stress, you help your body to embrace the treatment and allow the medication to work its healing. Researchers have found that even just ten minutes of Guided Imagery will reduce your blood pressure, lower your glucose and cholesterol levels, and heighten immune cell activity.

Getting Started

This book was originally written as a component of my Anti Cancer CD Set. The package included four CDs for which you'll find the actual script in a later chapter. The four CD's are:

Successful Surgery

Successful Chemo

Successful Sleep

The Healing Power of Your Mind

Whether you purchase my audio recordings or any other Guided Imagery recording, the following guide should help you get started.

Tips for best results

a) Find a quiet place free from distractions. Lie on the floor or recline in a chair. Loosen any tight clothing and remove glasses or contacts. Rest your hands in your lap or on the arms of the chair.

b) Take a few slow even breaths and exhale slowly. Breathe from your diaphragm, so that your lower belly or abdomen raises a little as you breathe in and fall back as you exhale. It may help to imagine a balloon inflating and deflating in your belly.

c) When you begin to feel the warmth of relaxation, gently close your eyes. This will help you focus your attention on what is being played.

d) Give yourself complete and full permission to release and let go. This is your time to heal and regain your strength.

e) You may become more relaxed than you are accustomed to being. Sometimes this may even feel as if you are a bit "out of control." Fine . . . the part of you that has been in control needs to let go a bit in order to allow the flexibility you need to change.

f) Don't worry if you find you have a stream of thoughts going through the back of your mind while you're listening. This is not uncommon, especially at first. Let the thoughts come and go, without paying them any particular attention. If you find your mind following a train of thought, just choose to let the thought go, focus again on what is being played, and move on.

g) Don't let your conditioned mind tell you that you are doing this wrong because you can't possibly "do it wrong". There is no one "right" way of practicing Guided Imagery. Everyone is different and this is why their experience may be different. Continue doing what feels good to you; it is exactly what's right for you at this time. Like any skill, learning and practice take time. Each time you listen you improve your skill and soon enough you'll be the expert.

h) You may notice some new sensations, perhaps a feeling of lightness, as if you could almost float or on the other hand, feel that your body is heavy or numb, and even some tingling in your hands. Enjoy these feelings and sensations and recognize that they reflect the positive inner changes that you are undergoing.

Clearly when you actively participate in your own care, you tend to feel better and do better... and that is why it is recommended that you listen to this audio program time and time again. The more you let your mind absorb the many special words, suggestions, images and metaphors fused into this program, the stronger and more healing its affect will be...

These special words, suggestions, images and metaphors will call upon your senses and imagination to engage your mind... so allow yourself, to become emotionally involved with each of them and experience their healing effect within your body.

If you hear a particular meaningful word or suggestion, or you enjoy a particular mental image or metaphor, allow yourself to linger over it, explore it and ignore the rest. It is worth your while to be creative as you listen, and rearrange a word or even a whole sentence as you see fit. Guided imagery is most effective when the words, suggestion and concepts that you hear become meaningful and personal to you, then, your mind absorbs their healing best, even when you are drifting in thoughts, which is common because of the dreamy state you are likely to be in.

It is common for people to drift in thoughts because they are not use to being both relaxed and awake at the same time. Let this worry you not, your mind is listening all the time, even when you drift toward sleep and comfort. It listens and absorbs what is being plaid and what is important. This is how we hear the alarm clock when it set off in the morning or a siren passing by.

As you listen, take only what is useful and leave the rest. If there's an image or a statement that is especially meaningful to you, try to briefly play it over, in your mind several times during the day, when you brush your teeth or stop for a red light or even better, just before falling asleep; this is an especially powerful time to do this.

The more you listen, the more you will begin to see yourself and feel yourself properly prepared, feeling confident, calm and relaxed. And as with any skill, practice makes perfect so commit yourself to this process of engaging the power of your imagination to help you heal and recover, to maximize the effectiveness of the medication and the treatment for your own wellbeing!

With that in mind, it is not necessary for you to listen to any of the introductions each and every time in order to benefit, though you can certainly do so when the need arise. Simply choose the CD and the track that is right for you, and allow yourself to become involved with what you hear, mentally, emotionally and physically.

CDs and Scripts:

Each CD or script begins with a phase of relaxation, followed by special words, suggestions, images and metaphors to engage your thoughts and imagination. The more you allow yourself to absorb these special words, suggestions, images and metaphors the stronger and more healing their affect will be.

You may find that your attention drift away or seems distracted by racing thoughts. If this happens, acknowledge these thoughts, set them aside and return your focus to what you read or what is being played.

The suggested images you read or hear are intended to be general enough for you to create your own details and sensations. You may even find your imagination to be a step or two ahead of my suggested images and that is perfectly fine. You may also find that as you relax, your muscles move or jerk. This is a normal and common experience for anyone experiencing stress or discomfort.

Sometimes, effective imagery generates an emotional response. If feelings arise, it's a sign that the imagery is working for you. Try to let the feelings pass through, your inner landscape as if they were white puffy clouds gently carried by the wind through the blue sky.

While guided imagery doesn't take long to learn, the more you practice, the more effective the benefits. Many people find it helpful to practice guided imagery twice a day, morning and evening.

The Successful Surgery

This audio CD is designed to help you prepare mentally and emotionally for a comfortable and successful surgery. It will also help you harness the power of your Mind for a speedy recovery. Each track is rich with information that will help you let go of fear and anxiety and develop a positive state of expectancy for a favorable outcome with minimal side effects.

Listening to these trucks on a daily basis you will find yourself feeling more relaxed and confident, more optimistic and at ease.

Listen to the CD regularly, at least once a day and avoid feeling apprehensive about the procedure. After your operation, keep on listing and provide your mind the roadmap for healing and wellbeing.

Script: Successful Preparation for Surgery

To begin this session... close your eyes... take a long deep cleansing breath and exhale slowly... take another long deep cleansing breath and this time as you exhale... allow you whole body to relax... your whole body, to relax...

Breathing in... and breathing out... relaxing with each and every breath...giving your mind and body complete and full permission to release... all and any tension you may be holding in your body....

And allow the warmth of relaxation that follows, to gently flow through each and every muscle, tended organ in your body... feel yourself relaxing and softening... any part that may feel tense to you, rigid or tight...

And as you do… you can wonder at the many ways you can experience this softness, and the release of tension all the way through, and all the way down your body…

And perhaps you can already feel the soothing warmth of relaxation, washing down any remnants of tension… from the top of your head, all the way down, to the very, end of your toes…

Gently bring your attention to your breath, and watch its rhythm … the rise and fall of your chest…

and notice how comfortable, and how good it feels to take in life this way… as you breath in… and as you breath out…

With each breath… allow yourself to focus inward more and more, to drift, ever so gently… into a place of true comfort and rest….

The further you drift, either in thoughts, in feelings or sensations, the better you feel… and the better you feel, the more calm, relaxed and comfortable you become…(more, and more, and more relaxed)

Breathing in… and breathing out… drifting further and further with each and every breath…

And you might wonder at this point… just exactly how calm and relaxed you could become, if you truly allowed yourself, permitted yourself to really let go…. how much more comfortable you could possibly feel if you journey further and further… into that deep and peaceful place within?

some people as they let go, may notice some tingling sensations, throughout their body, or some quality of lightness and light, as if they could almost float in ease, free from all things, just letting go… while others may feel some sort of numbness or heaviness in their body, as if they are shifting inward with ease into the center of comfort and calm within… all these feelings and sensations are very appropriate… and are perfectly fine…

they simply indicate to you that you are gently letting go, fully relaxing all the way through… doing exactly what you need be doing right now…

and if any thought comes to mind, any thought that shifts your focus elsewhere, away from feeling comfortable, safe and relaxed... release that thought with your breathe, as you exhale, so that your mind can be once again peaceful, free and clear...

When the mind is calm, and placid... still like the surface of a beautiful lake with no ripples... the body readily follows... and it too finds comfort and stillness, so much so that you may forget to remember it is even there at all... if this occurs it is perfectly fine, even expected... and then again, if your experience is somewhat different, this too is perfectly fine... simply observe, as if from afar, and accept this moment just as it is...

When the mind and body are so wonderfully relaxed, your imagination works wonders... so I would like you to visualize, see in your mind's eye, imagine if you will a special place... a place where you can feel truly safe and secure, calm and relaxed... like yourself again, free and at peace...

This can be a place you have visited long ago, a familiar one that has a special meaning to you... or a place you wish to create right now with your imagination, in your mind's eye...

Whichever you choose, let it be a place of true comfort and goodness, a place where you truly feel safe, peaceful and free... pause...

Take a moment to become aware of your surroundings, explore and allow this place of safety and healing to become more real and vivid for you, in all of its dimensions...

Try to sense how warm and comfortable you are, and how soothing and healing it may feel...

and in your mind's eye see its colors... smell its scents... and hear its sounds... birds, leafs, water... wind or music... just so that your ears can become attuned to the wonderful sounds of this special place, that is so safe and peaceful to you...

and as you become more and more aware of how safe and how beautiful this place really is, feeling thankful and happy to be there, you get that feeling of excitement again, that familiar sense, from deep within that something wonderful is about to happen...

You look around you and find a comfortable spot to rest in... a spot from which you can see in all directions and truly soak the beauty of this special place...

allow yourself to feel its peace... and as you drift in thoughts, let your awareness gently expand, and bring to mind all of those with whom you share a loving connection...

Sense how their genuine wishes for your wellbeing support you, and surround you with love...

Fully immerse yourself in this loving energy of support... feel it resonating within, warm and safe...

and as you do... let your awareness carry you forward in time... to the near future... to the time of your upcoming surgery.

With a sense of peaceful curiosity, see yourself, in your mind's eye in a clean and carefully prepared hospital room... laying comfortably on a soft bed, feeling good, safe, calm and centered...

this sense of calm and safety, is enhanced by the quality of the loving energy of support you have accepted, the connection you have with all of your loved ones... so much so that it fill the entire room, set forth the intent for a swift and comfortable procedure...

with your inner eye of understanding, you can see the experienced, confident and trustworthy medical team getting ready...reeling the equipment... making sure they have everything they need in order to offer you the care and healing that you seek...

It feels good to be surrounded by professional capable people who care about doing their work so well... You sense their skilled minds, and watch their caring hands making final preparations... they node to one another as if signaling that all is well and that they are ready for you...

And as the anesthesia begin to work, you become aware of some tingling sensation suggesting numbness and comfort... but just before you drift into comfort, you bring to mind the good faces of loved ones... seeing them wishing you well, smiling, pleased you have taken this necessary step to improve your health and wellbeing...

One of them looks steadily into your eyes and whisper quietly to you, I am so proud of you, proud of your courage and your determination to heal, you are an inspiration to us all...

And as these reassuring words lovingly echo in your ears, the sense of physical numbness takes over, throughout your body, ever so gently... like the warmth of a beautiful summer day...

You drift safely and easily into a deep state of comfort, as your body welcomes this numbness...

And still, your mind is calm, peaceful and aware... and with that awareness you watch as the team surrounding you, works over you... talking confidently, nodding to one another with satisfaction... expressing their surprise at how well things are going, how easy it is to do what's needed... and how cooperative your body is, even to the point of slowing down the flow of blood to treated area, to make their work go more smoothly...

Looking at their faces, you can tell they are content with the progress they are making... their hands move confidently and swiftly, like a beautiful choreographed dance from one place to another...

Your heart is filling with gratitude, for your body, for cooperating and embracing this surgery...

And this sense of gratitude grows and expands to include all those who wished you well; and further wish for your healing... You feel their loving, kind energy enveloping the whole of you... reinforcing your confidence and your determination to heal...

You hear the pleased murmur of the staff as they complete their work... mending... closing... healing... feeling good about what they have done... satisfied with themselves and with each other...

Your body is ready now, ready to heal... sensing the shift to recovery...

With that knowledge, you trust everything is now in place...and an image of yourself comes to mind... completely healthy and thriving... fully recovered

and your body waste no time at all, responding to this image, taking action, rapidly repairing itself... comfortably... and effortlessly...

your body's own innate intelligence, knows exactly what it needs to do...

new, strong and healthy cells are rushed to the site that is mending... weaved into place, creating new and healthy tissue, muscles and skin...

proper nourishment arrive diligently as well, supplying all the energy your body might need for swift and rapid healing...

Gently you are being moved to your resting room for recovery... and though your eyes are still closed... you can sense the presence of your loved ones in the room...

you hear their familiar gentle voices, and feel their warm and loving energy surrounding you from all directions, like a powerful shield so you can rest and gather your strength...

Slowly... you feel more and more present in your body, and everything feels just fine...

Ever so gently you rouse from your sleep, drowsy but comfortable... settled and calm... surprised to find the operation completed so fast...

You smile to yourself, and drift back to sleep, comfortably and safely as your body continue its healing...

In your mind's eye, you can see yourself active again, engaged in your favorite activity, moving freely, with grace and ease...

Your body is once again vibrant and strong and full of vitality... and you can move forward, in life, with a renewed sense of trust and respect for it...

You take a moment to be thankful, and celebrate the knowledge you were always safe throughout this procedure, always protected and cared for...

a tender wave of warmth and comfort surge through you, as if reminding you, there is so much for you to look forward to... dreams to realize... gifts to give, moments to be shared and enjoyed ...

Once again you reaffirm your decision and desire to heal...!

feeling something powerful has happened... and recognizing that a major shift has occurred, for the better, in your life... allow your thoughts to drift back, ever so gently, to your special place, the place from which you began this healing journey...

and once again become aware of your surrounding... the sights, the sounds and scents ...

and notice, notice how much more alive everything is... the colors are brighter, the sound are more pleasant and the air is filled with invigorating.... renewing.... rejuvenating...fresh scents...

This is your special place, and you can spend as much time here as you like... whether for comfort, for healing or to further the work you have already done... all you need to do is to close your eyes and wish yourself to be here, and you will...!

in a moment, as my voice gently fades away, you will have the choice to either bring yourself back fully, to the present time, into an awake state or continue to feel so wonderfully relaxed, possibly going even further and deeper, slipping into a soothing and restful sleep...

trust your mind and body to know what is right for you, what is most beneficial for you at this moment in time...

to bring your attention into the present time, count your way up, from one up to ten... and with each and every number feel yourself emerging safely... feeling good in every way... refreshed, energized and ready to go...

And then again if you wish to further deepen your sense of comfort and relaxation and slip into a long restful, peaceful sleep, count your way down, from ten to number one, and with each and every number, let your mind relax more and more... and after few numbers it doesn't take long all the numbers will begin to fade away and disappear... let that happen and enjoy your rest.

Regardless, know that you have done important healing work and that you are better for this now, and so you are...

Script: Successful Recovery from Surgery

To begin this session... as you settle down... close your eyes... take a long deep cleansing breath... and exhale slowly... take another long... deep cleansing breathe... and this time... as you exhale... allow your whole body to relax... your whole body, to relax...

Breathing in... and breathing out... giving yourself complete and full permission to release and let go of all and any tension you may be holding, throughout your body... your neck, your shoulders, your stomach...back...and legs... releasing all and any tension... and feeling your body softening... relaxing... finding comfort...

And as your body find its perfect rhythm of breath... note to yourself, that from this very moment, starting right now... each and every breath that you take... will serve to guide you gently but surely, (deeper and deeper) into a state of soothing... warm and comfortable relaxation...

This is your special time... to relax and support yourself, to take part in your own healing... and the more you allow your mind and body to engage and absorb what is being played, the faster you will heal and recover... and the more comfortable this journey will be...

Breathing in... and breathing out... feeling the warmth and comfort of relaxation flowing gently throughout your body... knowing that no matter how deeply relaxed you may feel as we go along... you can always go...that much deeper... and become... that much more relaxed... swiftly... and effortlessly... (easily... and effortlessly)the very act of breathing... the very sound of my voice will help guide you there with comfort and ease...

And to help you reach this warm, and pleasant feeling of comfort throughout your body... in a moment... I will count slowly... from 10... down to number 1... And you can count along with me... giving yourself complete and full permission to let go and drift further with each and every count... with each and every number... relaxing your mind... relaxing your body... finding comfort... with each and every count...

It doesn't really matter if you let go and relax quickly, or if it takes you a little longer to reach that deep and soothing place of comfort deep within...

Simply... focus on your breath as you count along... notice the rise and fall of your chest... and enjoy the subtle changes in your awareness... of how it feels to have every muscle, tendon and organ in your body softening, becoming so wonderfully relaxed...

The deeper you go the better you feel, and the better you feel, the deeper you go...more, and more, and more relaxed...

So very gently now, counting all the way down... starting with the number 10....(you feel safe & secure) 9...(you feel safe & secure) 8....(so relaxed now... so relaxed) 7...(so relaxed now... so relaxed) 6... (Peaceful... safe) (Calm & relaxed) 5... (You believe in yourself) 4...3... (Deeper &

deeper) 2... and finally number 1... so completely relaxed now... (More...... and more.......... and more relaxed...)

When the mind is calm, and placid... still like the surface of a lake with no ripples... the body too finds comfort... and at times you may even forget to remember it is there at all...

if this occurs this is perfectly fine, almost expected... and then again, if your experience at this present time is somewhat different, in any way, this too is perfectly fine... simply observe these experiences, as if from afar, and accept their shifting nature, the flow of feelings and sensations just as they are...

when the mind and body are so wonderfully relaxed, your imagination works wonders... so I would like you to visualize once again, imagine if you will, this very special place of yours... that is associated with tremendous feelings of peacefulness and tranquility....

See it taking shape in your mind's eyes, becoming more real and vivid, alive in all of its dimensions...

Feeling truly safe and secure... and with a childlike sense of curiosity... you become aware of your surroundings, and all the refreshing feelings of calm, contentment and happiness associated with this wonderful place...

Becoming more and more attuned with the healing property of this special place, feeling thankful and happy to be there, your attention is drawn outward by the playful dance of sun light on the ground, just ahead...

Moving into that spot of light and resting there for a just moment... You can feel the warm and soothing rays of light, gently caressing your face and body, emitting their soothing healing energy inward...

And breathing brings it into your body, more and more... so that each and every cell, gland and organ in it can be properly cleansed and nourished, strengthened and healed...

and maybe you can already sense this healing energy working within... strengthening the area of your body that is mending... supporting and restoring it back to health...

with each and every in breath, more and more light enters your body... flowing freely... dissolving anything that does not optimize your perfect health..., and every out breath... cleanses anything that does not promote your true wellbeing...

with a sense of wonder and gratitude you can feel this healing light flowing freely throughout your body... being absorbed by every cell, gland and organ in the area that is mending... and you accept this blessing... knowing this light does more than just heal the physical part of you, it also heal your mind... healing thoughts and emotions that are not in harmony with complete health and wellbeing, such as anger, shame, resentment and guilt...

All these pains must too be dissolved, for true and lasting healing to occur...

So simply sense, or just know that as the light moves through your mind and awareness... fear is neutralized and eliminated, helplessness is replaced with hope... and ancient grief is forgiven and released...

Feeling all throughout your body the cleansing power of this healing light... and feeling the shift on the inside, as your body aligns itself with harmonious thoughts and emotions, with hope and health...

This new awareness calms your heart and purifies your thoughts... allowing new energy to surge through you... revitalize, and replenish every molecule and cell in your body... encouraging and restoring its health... awakening the innate healing mechanisms into action...

And as this new energy flow... it cleanses and heals not only the physical part of you but also your mind... successfully stimulating it with new thoughts of health... with positive and powerful mental images of yourself, already healthy, recovered, strong, whole and healed... Pause...

Allow the softness of this awareness fills your whole being...and carry you forward in time... into the near future, perhaps two weeks from today... and see your incredible progress and how much you have already healed...

Feel the strength of your body... acknowledge its resilience and how well it has done its job...

You have more energy, greater mobility, you feel more invigorated and intact... optimistic and inspired to thrive and heal even more so than before...

Now see yourself even further in time, perhaps a month from today... and notice, notice how much better things are now... physically and emotionally, and in fact in every way...

In your mind's eye see your medical team pleased and, even surprised with your recovery and progress... pointing out to your rapid healing with satisfied approval gestures and words...

Now, let your awareness carry you even further now, to about three month from today... and feel yourself truly intact, whole again, like your normal self and even better...

It feels wonderful to be strong again, full of vitality, engaged in life... joyful and reassured...

With this newfound sense of joy, take a moment to be thankful, and celebrate the knowledge that in this moment, you are healing even more, making progress, doing exactly what you need to do...

And as you do, become aware of that tender wave of warmth and comfort that washes through you... lovingly reminding you, that there is so much for you to look forward to... many dreams to realize... precious gifts to give, treasured moments to be shared and enjoyed ...

acknowledging this, you reaffirm your decision to heal...you quietly but purposefully say to yourself ""My body heals quickly, easily and efficiently"

feeling something powerful has happened... you recognize a major shift has occurred, for the better physically, mentally and emotionally... and things will continue to develop and improve with or without your conscious effort to do so...for that is the nature of the healing operation within...

ever so gently, in a peaceful, and relaxed manner... bring your thoughts and awareness back to your special place... and let the sights, the sounds and scents come alive again in your mind's eye...

and notice, notice how much more alive everything is... the colors are brighter, the sound are more pleasant and the air is filled with invigorating.... renewing.... rejuvenating...fresh scents...

This is your special place, and you can spend as much time here as you like... whether for comfort, for healing or to further the work you have already done... all you need to do is to close your eyes and wish yourself here...

And so... in a moment, as my voice gently fades away, you will have the choice to either bring your thoughts and attention, to this present time, into an awake and comfortable state... or continue to feel so wonderfully relaxed, possibly going even deeper, into a soothing and restful natural sleep...

Simply trust your mind and body to know what is right for you...

to bring your attention back to this moment in time, simply count your way from number one up to number ten... and with each and every number feel yourself emerging safely...rising back to here and now, feeling good in every way... refreshed, energized and ready to go...

And then again if you wish to further deepen your relaxation and slip into a long restful, peaceful sleep, count your way down, from ten to number one, and with each and every number, let your mind relax more and more, and allow your body to follow... and after few numbers it doesn't take long, all the numbers will begin to fade away and disappear...

Regardless, know that you have done important healing work... that you are better for this, and so you are...

Successful Chemotherapy CD

This Guided Imagery audio program is designed to help you undergo chemotherapy more comfortably and heal more quickly with minimal side effects. The truth is that different people experience Chemotherapy in different ways and not everyone must cope with side effects.

This audio program aim to plant and nourish in your mind a new vision of health. It will help you develop positive expectancy for a favorable outcome. It is rich with suggestions and concepts that will support your state of wellbeing.

As we have discussed, you are able to play an active role in your journey toward health. And, you can maximize the effectiveness of the medicine by embracing it with a calm and prepared mind and body.

Script: Successful Chemotherapy

To begin this session... close your eyes... take a long deep cleansing breath and exhale slowly... take another long deep cleansing breath and this time as you exhale... allow you whole body to relax... your whole body, to relax...

Breathing in... and breathing out... relaxing with each and every breath...

giving your mind and body complete and full permission to release... all and any tension you may be holding in your body.... and feeling yourself relaxing... softening... releasing any part that may feel tense in any way, rigid or tight...

And as your body welcomes these new and comfortable sensations... you can wonder at the many ways you can experience this softness, and the release of tension from within...

And perhaps you can already feel the soothing warmth of relaxation, washing down any remnants of tension... all the way through and all the way down, from the top of your head, to the very, end of your toes... Pause

Gently bring your attention to your breath and watch its rhythm... the rise and fall of your chest... and notice, notice how comfortable, and how good it feels to take in life this way... as you breath in... and as you breath out...

With each breath... you allow yourself to focus inward more and more, and to drift, ever so gently... into a place of true comfort and rest....

The further you drift, either in thoughts, in feelings or sensations, the better you feel... and the better you feel, the more calm, relaxed and comfortable you become...

Breathing in... and breathing out... drifting further and further with each and every breath...

And you might wonder at this point... just exactly how calm and relaxed you could ultimately become, if you truly allowed yourself to let go and just be.... how much more comfortable you could possibly feel if you permitted yourself to journey further and further inward... into that central part of your mind and body, that place of inner harmony, and inner calm, or quiet stillness...

some people as they let go, may notice some tingling sensations, throughout their body, or some quality of lightness and light, as if they could almost float in ease, free from all things, just letting go... while others may feel some sort of numbness or heaviness in their body, as if they are sinking in a place of soft, velvety comfort... all these feelings and sensations are very appropriate... and are perfectly fine...

they simply indicate to you that you are gently letting go, fully relaxing all the way through... doing exactly what you need be doing right now...

and if any thought comes to mind, any thought that shifts your focus elsewhere, away from feeling comfortable, safe and relaxed... release it with your breathe, as you exhale, so that your mind can be once again peaceful, free and clear...

When the mind is calm, and placid... still like the surface of a beautiful lake with no ripples... the body readily follows... and it too finds comfort and stillness... so much so that at times, you may even forget to remember it is there at all... if this occurs this is perfectly fine, even expected... and then again, if your experience is somewhat different, this too is perfectly fine... simply observe what you feel as you go along, as if from afar, and accept this moment just as it is...

When the mind and body are so wonderfully relaxed, your imagination works wonders... so I would like you to visualize, see in your mind's eye, imagine if you will... a special place... a place where you can feel truly safe and secure, feel calm and relaxed... like yourself again, free and at peace...

The placed you envision can be a place you have visited long ago, a familiar one that has a special meaning to you... or a place you wish to create right now with your imagination, in your mind's eye... Whichever you choose, let it be a place of true comfort and goodness, a place where you can truly feel safe, peaceful and free... pause...

Take a moment to become aware of your surroundings, explore and allow this place of safety and healing to become more real and vivid for you, in all of its dimensions...

As you look around, note what you feel is special and meaningful, what is it about this place that makes you feel so good and comfortable?

in your mind's eye see the beauty of this place, see its colors... smell its scents... and hear its sounds... birds, leafs, water... wind or music...

and as you become more and more aware of how safe and peaceful and healing this place really is, feeling thankful and happy to be there, you see a pool of deep and clear refreshing water just ahead, a pool of life giving water, ever so pure and pristine...

The surface is calm and placid... perfectly reflecting the clear blue sky above... reflecting the beauty that surrounds you...

And looking into the pool, perhaps because the water is so pure and pristine, it's really hard to say... when one shade of color blends with the other... changing from the deepest blue... ever so gradually to turquoise, and finally to translucent green... blending so smoothly, flowing freely...

and there's something else as well inside that pool, something pleasant though quite unexpected, a special, white glow, coming from the water, illuminating the whole pool...

A sense of comfort washes over you as you look into that beautiful glow... your mind become still, still like the surface of the pool itself...

This wonderful glow fills your entire being with calm, making you feel truly safe and secure... and you get that sense again, that sense of sweet anticipation that something wonderful is just about to happen...

And no sooner than this realization sets in, you can see your reflection on the surface of the pool flooded with light and glowing...

Slowly you reach your hand, and touch the glowing water with your finger... creating ripples on the surface of the pool, ripples that flow gently and endlessly in all directions... meeting other ripples... creating magical shapes and forms that gently fade away ...

a soothing and pleasant sensation begin to flow into your finger as the light extends itself, from within the pool, ever so gently and comfortably, into the palm of your hand, your arm and you whole your body... flowing freely inward, into the deepest recesses of your being...

It is then that you realize that you have strength and courage you didn't even know you had...

And that there is a place within you, a central core of existence that is filled with harmony, with healing powers and life force which knew from the moment you came into this world how to heal scrapes and wounds and injuries, how to generate new cells and new tissue when needed... and how to regulate its own healthy functioning... your heart rate and breathing, your body temperature and blood pressure, all effortlessly, unconsciously and automatically...

This inner central core of existence is still within you and still working to heal you from the inside...

And as more and more light enter your body, it joins with this innate healing power... help it to mend and heal, and renew your body, effortlessly... applying a protective shield around the healthy cells of your body, especially your hair... digestive tract, your bone marrow, your heart and any other area that does not need to receive the effect of the medication...

In your mind's eye, see this healing power dissolving anything that is not in harmony with your perfect health, eliminating any abnormal cells or agents which do not fully promotes your true and lasting wellbeing...

this shield of light not only protect your vital organs, digestive system and hair follicles, it also purifies every drop of medication that enters your body... so that it can properly attach itself to only those cells in your body that are abnormal and need be dissolved...

and as the medication reaches those abnormal cells, it eliminates them rapidly, effectively and completely...

see this taking place as vividly as you can in your mind's eye, with your imagination... see those weak abnormal cells, shrivels up, dissolving and being released through the normal activity of your body...

and with your inner eye of understanding, visualize that healing light protecting every cell, fiber, gland and organ in your body... especially your scalp, and each and every hair follicle in it... strengthening and revitalizing the roots of your hair, shielding them from harm...

and then, see the medication agents, as they scour your entire system, identifying and eliminating anything that does not truly reflect your state of proper health...

With only your thoughts further direct this light through your body... see it shielding and protecting your esophagus... your stomach and intestines...

see it protecting your heart and even the cells in the marrow of your bones where new blood cells are being made, shielding them from the medication, enhancing their vitality and health...

Feeling all throughout your body the cleansing power of this healing glowing light...you embrace this moment... and the many blessings that it offers...

This new awareness stimulates your mind with a new vision of health, with positive thoughts and powerful mental images of yourself, already healthy, completely recovered, feeling strong and whole again... healed in every way... Pause...

Allow the richness of this awareness to resonate through the very fiber of your being...and carry you forward in time... into the near future, perhaps few weeks from today… and see in your mind's eye, the incredible progress that you have made…

You have more energy, and you feel more invigorated and intact… optimistic and inspired to thrive and heal, even more so than ever before…

With this newfound sense of comfort, take a moment to be thankful, and celebrate the knowledge that even as you listen and deposit what is being played in the treasury of your subconscious mind you are healing, making progress, doing exactly what you need to do…

you quietly but purposefully say to yourself ""in this moment I allow myself to heal, I am ready to have myself healed forever and ever, I really do"

and as the meaning of these words sink deep into your mind… you recognize that a major shift has occurred inside of you, for the better, physically, mentally and emotionally… and will continue to develop even further, with or without your conscious effort to do so…for that is the nature of the healing operation within us all…

ever so gently, in a peaceful, and relaxed manner... bring your thoughts and awareness back to your special place, and the pool of deep, clear and glowing water...

the surface of the pool are still placid but everything else seems so much more alive ... the colors are brighter, the sounds are more pleasant and the air is filled with invigorating.... renewing.... rejuvenating...fresh scents...

the healing light from within the pool is still within, helping you make progress, and will remain there for as long as you need... supporting, comforting and healing you as you go along... Pause...

now in a moment, as my voice gently fades away, you will have the choice to either bring your thoughts and attention, back to this present time, into an awake and comfortable state... or continue to feel so peaceful and so wonderfully relaxed, possibly going even deeper, into a soothing and restful natural sleep...

Simply trust your mind and body to know what is right for you...

to bring your attention back to this moment in time, simply count your way from number one up to number ten… and with each and every number feel yourself emerging safely…rising back to here and now, feeling good in every way… refreshed, energized and ready to go…

And then again if you wish to further deepen your relaxation and slip into a long restful, peaceful sleep, count your way down, from ten to number one, and with each and every number, let your mind relax more and more, and allow your body to follow… and after few numbers it doesn't take long, all the numbers will begin to fade away and disappear… Regardless, know that you have done important healing work… that you are better for this, and so you are…

Successful Sleep CD

This audio program is designed to help you calm your mind and calm your body so you can naturally and easily drift into deep and healing restful sleep. Using mental images, suggestions and metaphors it will help your mind re-learn how to let go and find comfort again. In doing so it not only allows you to sleep deeply and peacefully but it also enhances the quality of your sleep so you can wake up in the morning feeling refreshed and energized.

Sleep is fundamental to our health and wellbeing. It is a time in which the mind and body are engaged in the critical process of repair and restoration. We can harness the natural way of the body to heal itself to our advantage and this is what this audio will help you do.

Listen as you get ready to sleep and it will help you clear your mind and prepare for restorative rest. It will guide you through the steps of releasing stress and negativity so you can wake up feeling refreshed and at peace. It will help you create a night-time routine that allows you to quickly fall asleep and stay asleep throughout the night.

Script: Successful Sleep Script

To begin this session... close your eyes... take a long deep ...

Breathing in... and breathing out... relaxing with each and every breath...

giving your mind and body complete and full permission to release... all and any tension you may be holding in your body.... and feeling yourself relaxing... softening... releasing any part that may feel tense in any way, rigid or tight...

And as your body welcomes these new and comfortable sensations... you can wonder at the many ways you can experience this softness... experience this sense of comfort and release from within...

And perhaps you can already feel the soothing warmth of relaxation, washing down any remnants of tension… all the way through and all the way down, from the top of your head, to the very, end of your toes… Pause

Gently bring your attention to your breath and watch its rhythm… the rise and fall of your chest… and notice, notice how comfortable, and how good it feels to take in life this way… as you breath in… and as you breath out…

With each breath… you allow yourself to focus inward more and more, and to drift, ever so gently… into a place of true comfort and rest….

The further you drift, either in thoughts, in feelings or sensations, the better you feel… and the better you feel, the more calm, relaxed and comfortable you become…

Breathing in… and breathing out… drifting further and further with each and every breath…

And you might wonder at this point… just exactly how calm and relaxed you could ultimately become, if you truly allowed yourself to let go and just be…. how much more comfortable you could possibly feel if you permitted yourself to journey further and further inward… into that central part of your mind and body, that place of inner harmony, and inner calm, or quiet stillness...

some people as they let go, may notice some tingling sensations, throughout their body, or some quality of lightness and light, as if they could almost float in ease, free from all things, just letting go... while others may feel some sort of numbness or heaviness in their body, as if they are sinking in a place of soft, velvety comfort... all these feelings and sensations are very appropriate... and are perfectly fine...

they simply indicate to you that you are gently letting go, fully relaxing all the way through... doing exactly what you need be doing right now...

and if any thought comes to mind, any thought that shifts your focus elsewhere, away from feeling comfortable, safe and relaxed... release it with your breathe, as you exhale, so that your mind can be once again peaceful, free and clear...

When the mind is calm, and placid... still like the surface of a beautiful lake with no ripples... the body readily follows... and it too finds comfort and stillness... so much so that at times, you may even forget to remember it is there at all... if this occurs this is perfectly fine, even expected... and then again, if your experience is somewhat different, this too is perfectly fine... simply observe what you feel as you go along, as if from afar, and accept this moment just as it is...

Continue to breathe gently and allow the natural pattern of breathing to take over...

enjoying the feeling of letting go... of letting your mind drift here and there, calmly and effortlessly...

When the mind and body are so deeply relaxed, your imagination works wonder, so I would like you to visualize, see in your mind's eye, imagine if you will that you are standing in front of a blackboard... in one hand you have a chalk, and in the other an eraser...

Now in your mind's eye, see yourself drawing a perfect circle on the blackboard, of about 15 inches in diameter...

imagine writing the number 99 on the board in front of you.... and then wiping it out with your eraser, ever so gently, making sure not to disturb the circle or erase it in any way... and when it's done, and the circle is once again clear and clean, take a deep soothing breath, exhale, and notice how relaxed you can feel...

now do the same thing but this time imagine writing down the number 98 on the board, within the circle.... and notice, notice how you can relax a little bit more, as you erase the number carefully, and leave the circle clear and clean....in a moment, as I say the word begin, your task is to continue and write each number down, within the circle, one number follow the other... and each time you write a number and each time you erase it you can feel yourself become more and more relaxed.... more and more relaxed in every way...

so much so that you may find it becomes very challenging to remember which number comes next, or which number came last...and one before that...

the deeper you go the better you feel and the better you feel the more you remember to forget the numbers in their sequence... it will just seem so much easier to allow yourself to become more and more relaxed with each and every breath...

It may just be that you will notice more and more as you go along that even the number you are able to remember seem to fade away and disappear from your awareness, fade away and disappear into comfort, more and more... if that occur it is perfectly fine, even expected, and then again, if you choose to follow all the numbers, counting them down as you draw and erase them, this too is perfectly fine and you can continue to do so for as long as you need....

And all this time... while you continue to draw and erase... one letter after another... I will be talking in the background... and of course you will be able to hear my voice loud and clear, but you should pay no attention to it, what so ever... no attention at all...

begin this task right now, and see yourself in your mind's eye writing down, erasing, relaxing and letting go...

and regardless of whether you relax quickly or simply take your time to do so in a way that is comfortable for you, remember to pay no attention to my voice at all, despite of your ability to hear what it is that I am saying...

because when you think about falling asleep and staying asleep, there are many words you can be of help to you, many words that have something to do with sleeping peacefully throughout the night awaking refreshed and energized....

words like slumber and dozing and resting and snoozing are just a few of the many words that I can think of but you undoubtedly can think of many more, so go ahead and do that either now or later, or when later becomes now, it doesn't matter... you can think of many more I am sure... and keep the list in your mind, keep going over it as you think of more words and add them one by one or all at once to that list... and then make another one, another list of the many sounds that have something to do with sleeping properly, like snoring for example or breathing comfortably or even sighing... simply keep adding more and more sounds to that other list as your, even if you have to imagine what they sound like or whether or not you know a particular person who make exactly those sounds as they sleep, even if they sleep do deeply that they simply cannot hear anything at all...

As if that is not enough, bring to mind all sorts of images and things that have something to do with sleeping... things like pillows and blankets, duvets, slippers or warm milk... and collect those images into an imaginary album, in your mind's eye... adding more images to your collection each time you find one... adding them one by one, while hearing the sounds and reading the list of words and then add to that experience the feelings and sensations that have everything to do with sleeping.... comfortable and clean satin sheets, warm blankets, a loved one laying peacefully beside you... and add as many feelings as you can while you recite the lists and hear the sounds and see the images and feel the sensations on your skin and body...

It feels so nice to just let go, to let your body soften and relax, and let your mind become still, like the surface of a lake with no ripples... totally at ease, peaceful and relaxed... to know that there's a part of you... that really knows well... how to adjust to changes of the expected type... and perhaps even more important of the unexpected type... and I don't know if you have a name for that particular capability, a name or a label, or maybe it's a feeling that is simply familiar to you... or an image or something that you say to yourself... regardless of how it is known to you... you have utilized that part of you many times quite successfully to manage changes of all sorts in your life and you can do so again...

so you can enjoy that feeling.., and how to get to that feeling.., you can enjoy the confidence that things can change for the better and that they will change for the better...

and at times that you most want to or need to feel this way... you really can expect that feeling to be so strong and present in your awareness...

and it will occur in lots of different places, lots of different times... perhaps while listening to music, perhaps while thinking about things that you want more to enjoy and have in your life... perhaps while closing your eyes, just before you drift into sleep at night, or while planting seeds in the fertile ground of your own mind...

so you can expect the expected, and you can expect the unexpected... and you can expect consciously what your subconscious will not consciously expect... to have that expectation within you of what the future is all about... not as it is and not as if feels necessarily today, but rather of how much better things will be and feel tomorrow... and when tomorrow becomes today.., a day at a time.., and all the components are in place for you to enjoy a wonderful future experiences... then you can feel quite comfortable... quite energized...perhaps like your normal self again...

it's so comforting to know that the conscious mind has the freedom to drift...to imagine...to float through time and space to any wonderful place you desire...your mind can imagine all these things and so much more... and the fact is, it has already done so many times, even when you do not listen, even when your body relaxes and rest, here and now or over there...

When you get used to relaxing this way, time and time again, you will be pleasantly surprised to find yourself waking up in the morning and feeling so good, because the last thing you'll remember is breathing softly, or numbers fading away, or some lists that you have made of words, of feelings and sensations...

And once you know how it is so easy to drift away it just seems so natural.... there are some days when things are on your mind, and you wake up and sleep is fugitive, and that's OK... everyone has nights like that, it's just part of the normal cycle of life...

If that happens think of what you can do... you can get up, no point in lying there and do something quiet, that normally absorbs you... a hobby... reading a book... even looking through photos of loved ones...

and as you get absorbed in what you do, in whatever feels right in that moment in time, you will find yourself relaxing more... getting sleepier.... ready to go back to bed.... to a lovely warm and welcoming bed... and before you'll know, it is morning again and you are feeling refreshed, stretching leisurely... and remembering how you enjoyed that occasional night time interlude...

And you'll realize that deep deep restful sleep is a way thinking, a habit you enjoy, a way of experiencing what you enjoy about relaxing and letting go...

Some people get used to sleeping lightly.... or trying to stay alert... maybe they had a reason... and that's their mind doing what it can to keep them safe, which is a good thing of course...

you too enjoy that feeling of safety and security... that sense of comfort which help you relax and let go...

Day by day you are becoming more and more successful at feeding your mind with positive, comforting and relaxing thoughts... thoughts that will help you to enter that dreamy state, and drift swiftly and effortlessly into restful sleep...

And each day as you wake up in the morning, you'll have an inner feeling of excitement, a feeling of energy and underlying joy...

You will feel so good, refreshed, awake and centered, with energy and an inner feeling of comfort, health and wellbeing...and throughout the day, you'll hold onto that joy of living... and have abundance of energy to do anything you set your mind to do...

Let the richness of this awareness fill your heart with gratitude...and even carry you forward in time, perhaps to, tonight, or tomorrow night or the night after that...

In your mind's eye, see yourself lying in bed.... comfortably snoozing and dozing... drifting away.... into the warm and soothing feeling of sleep...

feel yourself lying there, satisfied and content... knowing that you no longer need to wonder any more if you will or will not easily fall asleep, that this was just a passing phase, and that now you are able to do that crazy thing called sleep any time you want...

just thinking about that makes you feel really good about the way you have helped yourself today... a little smile form in your mind, and you look forward to endless nights of dreamy peaceful and restful sleep...

just imagine yourself waking up in the morning, not long from now... having had a wonderful peaceful restful sleep.... many many hours of blissful restful sleep, feeling good in every way....

The Healing Power of Your Mind

Like all of our audio programs, this one is to be used in conjunction with your current medical care and treatment. Each track is rich with mental images, thoughts, emotions and feelings aimed to communicate with your mind and body in a way that helps stimulate and restore your body's natural healing ability.

Facing illness and treatment is challenging and demanding, and therefore, building a reservoir of inner strength, resiliency and courage is essential so we can meet these challenges with ease and comfort; and with a clear and positive mind.

This audio program is perfect for those looking for a more gentle approach to health, healing and recovery. It offers a pathway to an improved experience that is based on the knowledge that mind and body are in constant dialog.

You already know how important it is to condition your mind for a successful treatment, to cultivate a sense of mastery and feel and be prepared. Well, this audio program is designed to help you achieve all these goals.

When you set out to the clinic for your treatment, there is virtually nothing that you need to do physically to receive the treatment, except getting there that is. More or less, you just need to get yourself there and get through it, right? So very wrong, yet it is what most people do. Instead of spending time in constructive preparation, they engage in worry and fear and therefore fail to prepare mentally and emotionally for a successful procedure.

It is understandable, fear and anxiety, worry and concern will call upon the mind because any procedure is perceived as a threat. But just because it's understandable doesn't mean it's acceptable. You need not summon unimaginable powers to negate the effect of negativity; simply put the power of this audio recording to work for you. Use it before, during and after your treatment to ensure that you are completely ready to embrace its many blessings.

Script: Immune Enhancement

To begin this session... as you settle down... close your eyes... take a long deep cleansing breath... and exhale slowly...

take another long... deep cleansing breathe... and this time... as you exhale... allow your entire body to relax... all the way through and all the way down...X2

Breathing in... and breathing out.... Relaxing... as you breathe in.... (relaxing & letting go)

Relaxing...as you breathe out... (relaxing & letting go)

Noticing the natural rhythm of your breath... the rise and fall of your chest... the feeling of relaxation... as it gently now... begins to flow throughout your body... (Breathing in... breathing out...) from the top of your head... all the way down... to the very, end of your toes...

This is your special time to relax... and now... now is the perfect time for you to heal...

Breathing in...and breathing out... relaxing, with each and every breath...

Relaxing your neck and shoulders, relaxing your chest, stomach and back...

feeling your body softening... becoming, loose, limp and relaxed...(loose, limp and relaxed X 2)...

Feeling the warmth of relaxation... as it gently flows throughout your body... soothing...calming... and comforting...

But no matter how deeply relaxed you may feel right now or as we go along...you can always go that much deeper and become that much more relaxed... the very act of breathing... the very sound of my voice will help to guide you there safely and comfortably...

It doesn't really matter how quickly you may find yourself, so very deeply relaxed...

Simply... focus on your breath... (Breathing in... breathing out...) and give yourself complete and full permission to slow down... to relax... and let go...all the way through... and all the way down...

At this time... I would like you to visualize... see in your mind's eye... imagine if you will, that you are standing, in front of a black board...

In one hand you have a chalk... and in the other an eraser...

Now in a moment I would like you to draw a circle on the board in front of you... a perfect and crisp circle, of about 15 inches in diameter... and when you have... I would like you to draw, very carefully, inside the circle... the capital letter A...

Go ahead and draw the circle right now, in your mind's eye... and Make sure, to draw the letter A within the circle, without spoiling its perfect line in any way...

Once you have, imagine that you erase the letter A with your other hand... very carefully... and when the circle is once again clean... draw the capital letter B, at the same spot, inside the circle... but this time... I would like you to draw the letter B...backward, as if looking in a mirror...

Again, when you have... erase the letter B, very carefully without spoiling the circle in any way... and draw the capital letter C... backward... in a clear and clean line...

Now... in a moment, as I say the word BEGIN, and not before... your task is to continue and draw each capital letter in the alphabet... backward, within the circle............ until you reach the final letter Z...

however, after each and every letter... when the letter is erased and the circle once again clean... let your mind relax like your body is relaxed... let your mind relax just like your body is relaxed... and after few letter, because it doesn't take long... your mind too will feel so wonderfully and comfortably relaxed that all the letters will fade away, and disappear completely from your mind... easily and effortlessly...

So, go ahead, and BEGIN to draw the letters now... making sure to carefully draw them within the circle...

without going over, or erasing it in any way... this is very important.

And all this time... while you continue to draw and erase... one letter after another... I will be talking in the background... and of course... you will be able to hear my voice, loud and clear... but you should pay no attention to it... at least, not until all the letters have faded away from your mind...

Your task is to keep on drawing... drawing and erasing... one letter after the other... each letter that you draw... help your mind relax like your body is relaxed... and when all the letters have faded away... once again, bring your attention back to my voice...and allow my voice to guide you, ever so gently and safely, from this moment on...

Because it feels so good to just be, even for a moment... in a true state of comfort, where your mind is calm and your body with nothing to do... simply relaxes, and settle down...

Then...healing takes place... and the body begins to repair, and mend itself... one organ, gland and cell at a time...

There are of course many types of cells in your body... healthy ones which seem strong and round, vibrant and full of energy... and other cells which are feeble and sick... they seem week and even confused... as if not in place, not in harmony with the rest of the body...

Moment by moment, your body work to maintain its health... cells are being born... and cells that have done their job or cells that are ailing, they are being dissolved and destroyed by your innate and invigorated immune system that work within you, all the time...

It the same immune system that allow your body to overcome the flue, as well as heal cuts and scrapes, and even broken bones...

This, power to heal is innate... it was there for you from the moment you were born... and it is still within you, now, even today....

you see, we all have an active mind and a responsive body...meaning... that which you hold or imagine in your mind, naturally, take effect in your body, help your body heal...

And this time, right here and right now, you can begin to use this power to your advantage... use it, for the purpose of your healing and health...

Therefore see yourself in your mind's eye... imagine if you will that you can grow your body, ever so small, so physically small that it is actually possible for you to enter your body, and travel the inner realm of it...

imagined yourself becoming physically so tiny and so small that you can be carried through arteries and veins... carried by the blood stream... as if observing from a safe distance, and yet right there, very curious... feeling safe and protected... completely safe... feeling safe and secure...

By using your mind, your thoughts and feelings ... you have the power to navigate within, to influence, enhance and control every aspect of your physical body... and you can do so now, for the purpose of your healing...

you can use this power to activate, to revive and to strengthen your immune system... because remember now... you have an active mind and a responsive body... and when you focus your mind on health... and vitality... you are giving your brain the order to heal... and to restore health and balance to the body...

these mental images and thoughts that you uphold... tell your brain it's time to ignite, revive and boost your immune capacity... so that your body can once again work properly, as it was meant to work, and defend itself with ease and precision...

See yourself in your mind's eye, circulating through your body... and as you do... give your brain the order to release stronger and more effective white blood cells into your bloodstream... they are the healing agents of your immune system... and see them in your mind's eye represented by an animated or symbolic form... one that resonate with you... that represent abundance of energy, determination and strength...

Watch these healing agents stream through your bloodstream... full of energy and sure of their purpose, to dissolve any irregular cells or unhealthy growth that they may find...

With each breathe... you fuel your body, and strengthen your resolve to heal and overcome this challenge...

And as you breathe in and take in life... you reinforce your desire to recover, your desire to heal your body and heal your life... for that is your goal... the one goal that is so important to you...

The very decision to heal is invigorating... and you can use this energy to spark, ignite and encourage your immune system to perform with the outmost precision and fortitude... the way it is meant to work and perform...

You can feel your immune-system perk up and strengthen... and watch with gratitude as it sets forth to, identify and treat any abnormality or unhealthy growth that has come to be in your body...

And from your safe vantage point... see the powerful healing agents of your immune system identifying their target, which ever shape, form, color or texture that it may take, and see them approaching it...

see their target being treated by them.... And right before your eyes... see it, begin to dissolve... decapitate and heal... right before your eyes...

Let it happen now...right before your eyes... because now is the perfect time for you to heal...

You may be amazed at your body's resilience... and how it can properly target and treat, dissolve and heal any level of irregularity...

it does so, on a day to day basis, when you are awake... and when you are asleep...

This healthy activity within your body is ongoing, whether you are aware of it or not... and yet, right now...right now you are aware of it, and you can strengthen it... enhance it and boost it by focusing your mind, thoughts and feelings... thinking, feeling and seeing in your mind's eye the healing process as it unfolds...

And as you bring your attention once again to that area which your immune system found and treated... see it healthy, and completely healed... in your mind's eye...see it glowing with a healthy, pink glow ... see that area restored, soothed and healed...

Healthy blood is pumping through your body ... surging life through every vein, artery, gland and organ in it... giving you vitality and optimum health.

Your white blood cells are bursting with strength ... flowing freely in your body, patrolling it in a loving and protective way...

Watch how alert they are as they continue to search and scour your body of anything that does not optimize your perfect health...

Anything that does not optimize your perfect health is now easily eliminated... because your body easily differentiates between desirable cells and undesirable cells... and as it does... it cleanses itself of anything that does not support your perfect health... easily and with no ill effects...restoring you, and healing you... so you can once again enjoy feeling well, balanced and at peace...

Take a moment to visualize yourself, in a state of perfect health... where everything within you is functioning well and comfortably, effectively and efficiently...

and breathe this experience into your body... allow it to become a part of you, a part of your thought process, and let it become the truth about you...

Feel yourself glowing with vitality and purity... enjoying a renewed sense of wellbeing... a sense of hope, inner strength and inspiration that carry over, to the rest of your body... like a surge of energy that clear and heal any sort of imperfections or imbalances, anything that does not fully support your perfect health and wellbeing...

In this moment of renewed health... you feel soothed... nurtured, and protected...

you realize that this moment expands to include every other moment, every other moment from this time on...and you look forward to it, feeling better and better with every passing day...

See, and hear your loved ones celebrating your recovery with you... and notice how happy they are as they rejoice in your healing, celebrate your health...

it is as if you are bathed in warm soft light, held with love...from all directions...

Let these wonderful feelings and sensation be your experience...

let them become the truth about you... and as you do...

I am going to count from 1 up to number 5... and on the count of 5 and not before... bring your full attention back to this moment in time, let your eyes open... and find yourself feeling aware and alert... refreshed, charged, and ready to go...

1... emerging easily and gently... arteries expand and blood flow increasing...

2... feeling good in every way... feeling healthy from the inside out...

3... organs and glands functioning beautifully and properly... your body feel strong and alive...

4... your eyes clear beneath your eye lids, as if they have just been bathed in mountain fresh spring water... they sparkle with good...

And finally... number 5... bringing your full attention back to this moment in time... eyes open... fully open, and watches how good you feel...

Where Did It All Begin?

Guided Imagery has roots that date back to antiquity. In ancient Greek, the imagination was considered to be "an organ at the heart of healing" (Rossman & Bresler, 2003). Since that time, many other cultures around the world have found value in using imagery both for physical and psychological ailments.

In the twentieth century, social scientists and physiologists began looking back at the ancient wisdom once again. Attitudes slowly began to change among the general population as well as throughout the scientific and medical community. Pioneers like Freud (1900) and Jung (1964) came to the forefront of their fields. They wanted to discover more about the potential power of mental images and the unconscious mind.

As the twentieth century progressed, the scientific community became increasingly aware of these traditional therapies and slowly practices like Guided Imagery garnered more respect and interest.

In the United States, Guided Imagery really began to take hold in the scientific community during the 1970s. As practitioners found greater and greater success, they began using it in conjunction with other treatments for healing in general and cancer in particular. A radiation oncologist and a psychologist at the Cancer Counseling and Research Center in Dallas, Texas are considered to be pioneers within the industry. The Simontons, a husband-and-wife team who had been working in different areas of cancer care at the Cancer Counseling and Research Center, came together to research potential new treatments.

During their research in the late 1970s, they were shocked to discover all of the profound effects of relaxation and imagery techniques on patients. They saw improved quality of life and strengthened immune systems among the patients who were using imagery. Needless to say, this caused quite a stir within the research community. As you might imagine, people were shocked to discover how profound of an effect could be had from such a simple treatment. Of course, Guided Imagery is cannot and will not replace medical care but it can certainly help patients to better position themselves for healing. Even more so, it has no side effects or potential interactions with other treatments. It has long-term as well as short-term benefits. It seemed too good to be true.

Today Guided Imagery is being used for every possible ailment. People look to Guided Imagery to treat chronic pain, phobias, and hypertension among a host of other physical and mental conditions. That is not to say that Guided Imagery has not been dismissed at certain points in recent history. Of course, with each new discovery, there are always critics.

Some people believe that only drugs prescribed though a physician are effective while others vow to never touch them. Everyone views the world differently and wants to use their own unique approach to living in it. Some people will not believe the evidence placed in front of them while others will latch onto an idea without a shred of proof. While some doctors wholehearted believe in the critical nature of Guided Imagery in the healing process, others are completely unaware of its potential benefits. Slowly, over the past few decades, it has taken hold in the medical community. Doctors are recommending it and patients are requesting it.

There is now an entire field of science called psycho-oncology that focuses its attention on the critical nature of the mind. They are working to progress our understanding, and consequently our ability to utilize, things like Guided Imagery in cancer care. They draw their inspiration from a vast range of psychological therapies. They look into the valuable features of humanistic psychotherapy, cognitive behavioral therapy, and transpersonal psychotherapies among many other tools that the medical community had developed over the past century. By combining ancient wisdom with modern practices, they strive to create the best possible solutions in cancer care. It is definitely an exciting area of cancer care research to watch.

We do not know where the future will take us but those of us who have been practicing Guided Imagery for many years feel that we are on the right path. Cancer is a serious issue that needs to be tackled on all fronts. We believe that as research continues, the medical community will be able to make dramatic strides. By creating an ideal mixture of modern medical science, ancient wisdom, and advancements in our understanding of psychology, the medical community is making cancer care increasing personalized and more effective.

How Is GI Utilized in Cancer Care?

Guided Imagery is one of the most frequently recommended complementary therapies for a cancer (Schmidt and Ernest, 2004). It is used to calm patients and reduce their anxiety which can, in turn, reduce pain. It is also believed that it can help to speed up the recovery process. (Simonton et al., 1978)

Guided imagery stimulates the parasympathetic part of our nervous system. This is the portion of our nervous system that induces various "rest-and-digest" activities and "fight-or-flight" responses. It is only when the body is at rest that healing can take place. We often exhaust our bodies by feeding our nervous system with a constant stream of stressors.

The primary goal of Guided Imagery is to increase our ability to deal with stressors, and in turn, lessen the effect that they have on our bodies and nervous systems. Of course, reducing stress has an immediate effect on our mood but, as you now know, it is about much more than that. When we find a way to relax our minds, we also relax our bodies. This relaxation is an integral part of allowing our bodies to work through the healing process. Increased stress levels can only have negative consequences on our health.

Reducing stress levels is the primary goal of those practitioners who use Guided Imagery in cancer care. Using Guided Imagery effectively is a skill that we aim to teach in order to allow patients to relax the entirety of their beings. When using the program, your attention will be guided to a voice and a series of sounds and rhythms. The carefully constructed script used in the program will offer you transcendence away from your body and illness. By transcending your body, you are able to remove yourself from its pain and stress and allow it to utilize its energy for repair and healing.

Guided Imagery is a profound experience because it allows to you feel cultivate mastery over your body. One of the most valuable things that you can do for yourself is learn to gain a feeling of control over your experience. The more power that you feel that you exert over your body and your circumstances, the more in control you will be. These feeling of empowerment have a deep, lasting effect on us psychologically and physically. Feelings of helplessness have been consistently shown to correlate with slowed recovery and increased distress. In other words, your body and mind wants you to feel in control. When you believe that you are in control, you are able to thrive on every level.

Feeling overwhelmed or afraid is completely natural and instinctual, especially when faced with a major life change or a difficult struggle. It is not a sign of weakness or an indication that one cannot handle the stress of the disease. While people often like to tell stories about those unique individuals who are strong or label people as "fighters," these are not unique traits. We all possess the instinctual drive to keep ourselves healthy and we will always fight to stay alive.

Many people have told me that they just didn't feel like they were up for the "fight." They felt exhausted by the idea of beginning cancer care. They felt like their diagnosis was a death sentence and that they felt like they were victims. The important thing to realize is that we all feel this way sometimes. This is true in every aspect of life, not just in the area of cancer care. There are times when each and every one of us felt like we are not strong enough to face our problems.

It is so important to remember that these feelings are very natural and completely human. When we talk about feelings of helplessness or empowerment, we are not talking about concrete traits. We may all have certain tendencies but they are all within our power to change. There are no weak or strong people. What separates people, however, is their willingness to overturn these emotions of helplessness and despair into empowerment and hope.

If you can work though through these negative emotions or even simply set them aside for a moment, you will find your life can slowly become dramatically different. It may even feel false at first and that's okay. You may have heard the expression "fake it until you make it." I think this statement can be applied to everything. You might not feel empowered when you take your first step but that does not truly matter.

Once you begin taking the steps toward empowerment, you will slowly begin to feel more confident. This is really one of the keys to everything. Even if you don't feel like you are the sort of person who would typically use meditation or Guided Imagery, don't let that dissuade you. Everything is new the first time we try it and, until you try something, you never know what you might enjoy. This is important advice because it is empowering advice. It is important that you feel ready and able to fight against stress.

When a person is under stress, their body reacts to it. Their limbic system suppresses their immunity, which makes people more apt to get cancer and prolongs the course of the disease. Researchers have found that those with Type C personalities, which are marked by traits of helplessness, passivity, and a tendency to suppress anger, are more likely to have more invasive tumors (Temoshok, 1987). It is a very powerful idea if you spend a moment thinking it over. On first glance, it seems easy to dismiss the notion of changing your attitude in order to change your body. Scientists and researchers, however, have found strong correlations between people's attitude and their health.

One of the things that researchers are finding over and over is that those who believe that they have a high level of control over their lives are better able to respond to fight disease. In other words, if your brain tells your body that you can't fight against illnesses; your body won't fight against the illness.

It's quite amazing really to realize that your brain can motivate your body into action. Of course, our bodies are extremely complicated tools so there is a bit more to it than that but it's a very important idea. While a positive attitude cannot change everything, research is making it clear that a negative attitude will almost surely exacerbate conditions.

This connection between the mind and body can be clearly seen in the case of long-term stress. When a person is under chronic stress their body releases an excess of corticosteroids. This causes a chain reaction that ultimately reduces the immune system's ability to fight diseases. You may have even found this in your daily life. When you are under stress, you tend to feel a bit worse. You might find yourself starting to sleep less and become more prone to colds and headaches and even just getting upset.

One of the primary goals of Guided Imagery is to bring the mind to a deeper state of calm. We know that when you are in this deeper state, your mind has an increased sensitivity toward positive images. These images are used by your brain as biochemical signals that are sent from the cortex and limbic system. They release hormones into your autonomic nervous system, which uses them to control your breathing, blood pressure, and heart rate. When you are facing cancer, these effects can greatly increase your ability to heal and fight the disease.

By examining this effect on the cortex and limbic system, researchers have been able to find a clear, physical effect with Guided Imagery. By studying patients using Guided Imagery with positron emission tomography (PET) and functional magnetic resonance imaging (fMRI), they were able to see the clear physical effects. They found that "imagery of emotional events activates the autonomic nervous system and the amygdala." In other words, they found that "visualizing an object has much the same effect on the body as actually seeing the object" (Kosslyn, Ganis & Thompson, 2001).

I have discussed this idea many times because I find it to be so spectacular. We can participate in an event, any event that we can possible imagine, without moving a muscle. Imagine sitting through an uncomfortable treatment or waiting to go in for a stressful surgery. You know how overwhelmed your mind feels at times like this. It is exhausting just to think about having to go through the experiences. Now imagine having the ability to remove yourself from these situations anytime you want. Of course, you can't really physically remove yourself but you can transcend the circumstances. You can allow your mind to drift away to any place that you prefer. Once you learn how to effectively used Guided Imagery, it is at your disposal anytime and anywhere.

One of the major issues faced by physicians working in cancer care is that their patients simply do not want to do the treatments. They are afraid of how they would feel and look. If they do press forward, many will schedule and re-schedule appointments simply because their nerves are keeping them away from doing what they know they need to do. Guided Imagery has helped many patients who had previously been doing exactly this overcome their fear and complete their course of treatment.

How Can GI Benefit Cancer Patients?

As I have discussed, Guided Imagery is highly effective and offers many benefits in cancer care. With only ten minutes of Guided Imagery, you can feel more confident, more prepared and less anxious, speed up recovery and healing and even increase your immune cell activity. Even more so, you can lessen headaches, ease depression, turn nausea to healthy hunger and fatigue to vitality. It may sound like the effects of a miracle drug but it is totally natural. If you learn to harness you mind's natural ability, you can really transform your life and learn to manage your cancer.

All this can be achieved because Guided Imagery override cognition and allow your mind to communicate directly (and unconsciously) with your body. Imagery is received through feelings and sensations rather than analyzing and deciding. As a cancer patient, Guided Imagery can help you see through your treatment. It can help you maximize the effectiveness of your medical treatment and in doing so increase your odds for recovery.

In 1978, radiation oncologist Dr. Carl Simonton examined the effects of Guided Imagery by studying patients over a four year period. Amazingly, when the results were being published, he had found that the still-living patients who had utilized guided imagery lived, on average, twice as long as those who had solely received standard medical treatment. While there are no guarantees in life, those can only be seen as encouraging results.

Imagine if I told you that you had the potential to increase your lifespan so dramatically simply by closing your eyes and relaxing. It seems impossibly simple yet, at the same time, we know how difficult true relaxation can be to achieve. Even with good intentions, we often become too busy and procrastinate.

Of course, it is easy to get together everything you need to begin a Guided Imagery program but how difficult is it to actually do it on a consistent basis? On one hand, it is very simple. You just set aside a few minutes per day and listen to the program. It should be as easy as watching your favorite television program. At the same time, however, it is extremely difficult to develop new habits once we are set in our ways. It is so easy to say that we will start something tomorrow or that we will just skip our new routine for one day. I strongly encourage you to avoid this type of thinking. You have read how profound Guided Imagery can affect your cancer care treatment and quality of life. If you use this knowledge and consistently follow the program, you are giving yourself a true gift.

Another study in 1988 done at the Medical Illness Counseling Center in Maryland found that Guided Imagery increased white blood cells and allowed the body to better fight against cancer cells. They also found that Guided Imagery helped with pain management, pre- and post-surgical procedures, and promote the general well-being among numerous other benefits. These benefits can aid patients long after their cancer care is complete. You don't need to have cancer for Guided Imagery to positively impact your health and well-being. Long after cancer, you can use it to prevent and manage any type of physical or mental ailment.

While researching the effects of Guided Imagery, Dr. Remen, the director of Commonwealth, a health research center, talked to patient who reported having "vividly experienced 93 surgeries." He had only had three operations but could clearly recall the details of 91 other imagined surgeries. I can't tell you how it pained me to read his story. I think it is something that we can all easily relate to on many levels. Even from childhood, we have a tendency to dread and relive experiences in our minds over and over. We imagine ourselves going through dreadful experiences so many times before they even happen. Sometimes these dreadful experiences never actually end of happening. We have caused ourselves such a great deal of stress for nothing.

On the other side of things, if something stressful does happen we feel that we must live it over and over. It does not matter how trivial the event was, we feel compelled to replay it in our minds again and again. Of course, there are times when we can use this to learn from our past mistakes but often it only results in stress. In order to thrive in our lives and be able to bounce back from trying times, we need to do everything in our power to fight against this tendency. Therefore, the next time when you are spending your energy to image and relive stress events, try Guided Imagery. Try to reverse this pattern by putting your mind at east before a difficult time. After stressful events, use Guided Imagery to push the negative memories away. You will be shocked to see what a profound and lasting change it makes.

Like I mentioned earlier, research has shown us that our brains do not truly distinguish between the events that we imagine and those that actually take place. If you are dreading an event and keep picturing it in your mind, it is as if you are having the event take place over and over. Similarly, if something traumatic or stressful has happened and you continue to dwell on it, you are causing your brain to relive the experience time after time. This type of stress is bad for you psychologically and physically. It is bad enough to have to live through certain events one time, say nothing repeating them again and again. One thing that Guided Imagery can help you do is let go of these thoughts.

Studies have shown that emotional depression suppresses the immune system. When presented with negative imagery, the body will undergo a negative cardiovascular change. However, when presented with positive imagery, like that used in Guided Imagery, the body will have a positive reaction (Achterberg, 1985).

Over the course of many years, doctors have noticed that patients who experience a medical crisis will often turn to spirituality. You may have even noticed this in your own life. When you are forced to face your mortality, you begin to start thinking more existentially. Religion can offer a great deal of solace during trying time for some. Guided Imagery can enhance this or offer deeper meaning on its own.

Like most aspects of life, Guided Imagery also has a financial side. It has been noted that patients experiencing emotional distress of any form require more visits to the doctor and are hospitalized more often. Patients are often visiting their physicians even when there is no apparent physical issue. A recent three and half year study of

Medicaid patients found that 80 percent of costs were associated with only 20 percent of Medicaid users. After introducing this group to relaxing techniques, each of participants were able to save more than $85 in just six months (Mental Medicine Update: The Mind/Body Health Newsletter IV(4), 1995). Of course, I believe that this just goes to show what a profound effect the mind has on the body. It is often difficult to truly see if we are facing physical symptoms or are under emotional distress.

While some amount of discomfort and distress is nearly inevitable when working to manage cancer, there is so much that you can do to make your journey easier. While it may sound intimidating to try to learn a new skill while during a hectic time in your life, don't let that discourage you. Guided Imagery is similar than you may be imagining. All you need to do is relax. There is nothing more to it. Just begin listening to the program and allow it to

What Research Has Been Done on GI?

As I have mentioned throughout this e-Book, a wealth of research has been done on the topic of Guided Imagery. When I first discovered the topic, I was amazed by the quantity and quality of research that I have found. It was nothing short of inspiring to learn the mind, my mind could have such a profound impact on my body and that it can help me and support me. This was nothing I learned about or knew about before.

One research I found focused on patients in early stages of melanoma. Researchers found that after six months of using Guided Imagery their moods were significantly more positive and their had increased their bodies' ability to fight the disease. Another study done on breast cancer patients showed that those who had learned and practiced Guided Imagery greatly benefited from the technique. On average, they lived significantly longer than those who were receiving standard medical treatment alone (Malignant Melanoma: Effects of Early Unstructured Psychiatric Intervention; Recurrence and Survival 6 Years Later. Archives of General Psychiatry: 1003;50).

In spite of all of the research, scientists are yet to uncovered the exact reasons as to why Guided Imagery is so effective. We do know that the foundation of Guided Imagery is based around carefully planned narratives that send neurohormones, activated in the nervous system, through the circulatory system. We know how the relaxation techniques work with the body but researchers are yet to prove conclusively why they do so.

As we have discussed, the Simontons were really the leaders in the area of Guided Imagery. The husband-and-wife team at the Cancer Counseling and Research Center in Dallas, Texas paved the way for those who would follow. After their initial discoveries in the late 1970s, they joined with other researcher to look into the true potential of Guided Imagery. They eventually joined forces with another husband-and-wife team, Achterberg-Lawlis. Together they developed a diagnostic test, which they tagged the Image CA. The test evaluates cancer patients' imagery and assists in making a prognosis. They test has been used since then to assess Guided Imagery's ability to aid in cancer care.

Beyond just looking at the physical effects of Guided Imagery, a great deal of research has been done to evaluate its effect on overall comfort level. As those of us battling cancer are very aware of, one's comfort level is paramount. Of course, the long-term physical progress is important but, some days, there is nothing that we want more than to simply be comfortable.

At the end of the twentieth century, a comprehensive study was done on Guided Imagery's impact on comfort level. Kolcaba and Fox (1999) had studied Stage 1 and 2 breast cancer patients to see exactly what sort of impact Guided Imagery could have. Kolcaba and Fox summarized their findings by saying they found "a complex outcome relating to the human needs for relief, ease, and transcendence within the physical, social, psycho-spiritual, and environmental concerns." In simply terms, the patients felt much better on every level after they began using Guided Imagery.

A similar study was completed a few years later to test the effects of music and Guided Imagery on a range of cancer patients and similar results were found. Researchers found that the patients were scoring lower in depression assessments and reported a higher quality of life following the treatment (Burns, 2001). In both cases, it took nothing more than learning to utilize relaxing imagery to make a marked increase in patients' levels of happiness and contentment.

In order to further investigate the physical aspects of treatment, researchers have also looked into how stress impacts cancer treatment. It has been hypothesized that those patients who are experiencing stress will have poor responses to chemotherapy (Walker et al, 1999). Of course, as a cancer patient, you know that stress is an automatic response to any sort of intense treatment let alone chemotherapy. Being diagnosed with cancer will automatically increase anyone's stress level. These are obvious fact but the more complex question is: what can we do about it? If cancer causes stress and we can't fight cancer well when under stress, what can we do? Of course, I believe Guided Imagery is a critical part of this equation. It will advance the quality of your life, strengthen your resolve to heal and recover and set you on a course for improved outcome.

In addition to just proving the theory that Guided Imagery reduces stress, fear and anxiety researchers of another study went further to declare that their findings "supports the importance of psychological factors as independent predictors of response to primary chemotherapy" (Walker et al, 1999). They believe that Guided Imagery not only increases patient comfort levels but also increases their ability to successfully receive cancer care through chemotherapy. Needless to say, this was considered to be a very bold statement.

This suggests that Guided Imagery help us not only to cope emotionally, it also aids us physically. And as I have mentioned, it only takes some ten minutes to gain a positive impact. How many other tools or things we can say do that? We can take a pill in one second, which may help with easing the discomfort of treatment physical side effects, but it won't help ease the emotional ones.

Researchers have found that many patients are initially drawn to Guided Imagery to help them with their anxiety and pain. Patients in cancer care often feel overwhelmed by the emotions and physical discomfort that come with the illness and the treatment. They grow increasingly desperate to find solutions and one successful solution they employ is Guided Imagery.

Several years ago, a group of researchers hypothesized that people suffering from pain feel a disconnection between their minds and bodies. When we are suffering from intense or chronic pain, we have a tendency to want to pull our minds away from our bodies. A study done in 2000 by Moore and Spiegel investigated Guided Imagery's ability to recreate the connection between the mind and the body. This is a critical link that is often broken during times of illness and pain. It is believed that imagery can be used to connect the mind and body and allow patients to make some sense of their physically experiences. This also aids patient's ability to empower themselves.

When we feel that our body is a distant mystery, we don't believe that we can harness any control over it. We can only look to escape when we feel that we don't have any power. This is not productive in cancer care. As I have been stressing, self-empowerment is key to successful treatment. It aids our body in the healing process and keeps our mind at ease.

Cancer is an epidemic not just here in the US but throughout the world and researchers everywhere search for effective ways to win over this illness. While progress is evident we the end is not in sight.

Numerous studies have taken a closer look at each potential consequence of Guided Imagery. After telling you about the results of so many studies, let me tell you about a particular study in a bit more detail. It is easy to nod our head at the published results but it is more helpful to hear exactly how Guided Imagery is used in these studies. Let me tell you more about a recent study done on a group of cancer patients in South Africa.

This recent study hypothesized that Guided Imagery would decrease systolic blood pressure, overt anxiety, diastolic blood pressure, and anxiety. However, in addition, to these positive side impacts, they also hypothesized that Guided Imagery would not result in a significant decrease in depression.

The participants in their study were patients facing Stages 1, 2, and 3 Cancer. The patients were divided into two groups: the experimental group and the control group. Before beginning the study, they tested each group to see if they were starting with similar levels of systolic blood pressure, overt anxiety, diastolic blood pressure, and anxiety. There were predictable variations in physical and psychological test result levels between patients but they found similar average levels between the two groups.

The entire group of participants was comprised of 30 different cancer patients, who were split up into the two groups. Their ages ranged from between 30-75 years old with the mean age being 60. They had varying backgrounds and support networks. The men and women were recruited from cancer treatment facilities around Johannesburg, South Africa. As a group, they were suffering from breast, endometrial, vulva, larynx, cervical, prostate, tonsil, and thyroid cancers.

In order to test the results of Guided Imagery, the researchers used the Hospital Anxiety and Depression (HAD) Scale. The HAD scale is a self-rating questionnaire that was developed to detect affective disorders. Clinics at cancer care facilities have long been concerned with patients' likelihood of developing anxiety or depression after a cancer diagnosis. The HAD Scale is one tool that they use to check on patients' psychological health rather than just focusing on their physical health.

The researchers also used the Institute for Personality and Ability Testing (IPAT) Anxiety Scale. The IPAT test is also self-reporting and is used to measure overt, or conscious, anxiety as well as covert anxiety. In other words, they wanted to see how much anxiety the patients knew that they were experiencing while also testing for other sings of anxiety that they may not being fully realizing on conscious level.

Finally, the researchers also utilized the Multidimensional Health Locus of Control (MCLC) Scale. This test assesses a person's perceived level of control. As we have discussed, things like helplessness and self-empowerment can have profound consequences on a person's physical and mental health. In addition to these factors, the MCLC Scale also looks at things such as a person's views on fate, luck, and chance. Basically, the scale helps researchers to establish exactly what level of control patients feel that they have over the course of their illness. Patients who feel that they can control their illness may respond to every part of their treatment differently from those who feel that they are at the whim of fate. If a patient believes that they have little or no say in their treatment, they will also have a very different experience from the patient who believes that he or she is in full control.

These tools were combined together to help give researchers a clearer view of each participant's psychological health before and after the study. Standard measures of blood pressure, both systolic and diastolic, were taken before and after the experiment to see whether or not Guided Imagery was able have any impact on the levels.

During the research study in Johannesburg, every patient was provided with free access to a social worker. In addition to this, the patients in the experimental group were also instructed on Guided Imagery. They were taught relaxation techniques and were also taught how to use these same techniques on their own whenever they felt like it. They were instructed to use their Guided Imagery program at least once a day. The experiment lasted for 12 weeks. The experimental and control groups were both tested four times throughout the experiment on the MHLC exam so that researchers could gauge their mental health.

The participants who used Guided Imagery developed a "safe place," where they could take their mind whenever they needed to relax and get away from the pressures of everyday life. In their sessions, they talked about how they had envisioned their healing. Some people believed that a religious figure would help them fight cancer while others thought that their inner strength would ultimately make them healthy again. As you might expect to find with any group as large as 15 people, there were many variations in their responses to the treatment. Some were diligent about using Guided Imagery while others had times where they just could not fit it into their schedules.

Despite these individual differences, there were consistent findings within the experimental group who had used Guided Imagery. At the end of the study, researchers found significant improvements in diastolic blood pressure, covert anxiety as well as general anxiety, and depression levels within the experiment group. They found few changes in the control group. In other words, those participants who had been instructed on Guided Imagery were able to reduce their blood pressure and anxiety while reducing their depression. These results were actually better than the original hypotheses had projected since the researchers were not expecting to find a reduction in depression levels.

These results were realized only within the 12 week period during which the research took place. During conversations with the patients, those who were experimenting with Guided Imagery felt that they had gained a greater sense of control over their lives (Campbell-Gillies, 2005).

There is nothing unique about this study but I think it serves to provide you with a better picture of what exactly all of these researchers' results mean. Bear in mind that the participants of this study were only asked to use Guided Imagery for a few minutes per day over the course of three months. They did not need to sit in a hospital for their treatment and it was not a skill that they need to learn how to harness over many years. It was a very manageable change that they were able to make in their lives and, as a result, they found significant improvements in their health and wellbeing.

How to Put Everything into Practice

As I've said, one of the most valuable gifts that you can give yourself is self-empowerment and self-mastery. If you are engaged in the process of your care, you can lessen your discomfort. You have already taken the first step by reading through this book. From here, each one of our audio programs will tell you exactly what to do. All you need is an open mind and the desire to heal. In order to get more familiar with the experience, you may want to designate a place in your home where you will be comfortable and hopefully will not be disturbed. Then you can settle down and begin listening to whichever program you choose.

Your Guided Imagery program will walk you through every step on the process. You don't need to worry about doing it incorrectly. There is no right or wrong way of going about it. The worst thing you can do is to not make the effort. As long as you keep coming back to the program day by day, you will feel the impact. Just begin playing the audio and allow yourself to be gently guided, become immersed with what is being played. The more you listen and practice, the more effective you will find the program.

You have already taken the most important step by deciding to play an active role in your care. As we have discussed, this simple act will empower you and strengthen your resolve to heal. When you believe that you are in control of your life and your destiny, everything changes for the better.

Rather than sitting back and waiting for help or, even worse, declaring that help will never come or that there is no hope, you are being proactive. You have chosen a path in which all of the doors are open to you. This is a critical mindset when you are facing the challenges of treatment. It is also a skill and way of thinking that will serve you well long after your battle with cancer has finished. Those who have empowered themselves and feel that they are in control of their lives will find every aspect of life to be more manageable. I hope that after you learn the skills of Imagery, you continue to use them in your everyday life whenever you are facing a challenge or just need to put your mind at ease.

So how do you learn these skills? Well, through this program. Simply sit back and relax in the same manner that you would if you were preparing to listen to your favorite music. When you are listening to music, you don't need to concentrate deeply to take in all of the words and sounds. When you listen to a song a few times, you suddenly realize that you can start to sing along with parts of it. The more you listen to the song, the more you remember. You would never sit down with a pen and paper and take notes about song. You don't need to do this because listening and picking up information comes innately to us.

Do not think of your Guided Imagery program as an exercise in listening. There will be no exam afterwards and you don't need to feel anxious about doing any portion of it wrong. Just relax and listen to the narration, it is designed to quiet your mind and help you enter into a heightened state of relaxation and comfort

Both your body and mind want to relax. Out of habit, your brain might put up a bit of a fight but it will not last for long. Soon you will find your mind craving the relaxation. We tend to forget how necessary and natural relaxation is for us. As a culture, we tend to confuse the concepts of laziness and relaxation and think that we always need to be busy.

About the Author

Avinoam Lerner is a holistic therapist and the author of *The New Cancer Paradigm – Increase the Effectiveness of Your Medical Treatment with Immersive Healing*.

His innovative approach to cancer recovery highlights the multidimensional nature of our being and the need to treat illness not only on the level of the body but also on the level of Mind. He offer patients seeking to play a more active role in their care, a practical, meaningful and effective path to engage the creative power of their Mind to revive their body's innate immune response and strengthen its capacity to defend and fight cancer.

Avinoam guiding belief is that for true and lasting recovery we must transcend the mechanistic-reductionist-Newtonian view of disease and recognize that illness is a whole person event. As such he works with patients in all stages at his Watertown MA private practice to strengthen their body's innate immune response, increase physical and psychological resiliency and enhance their outlook and attitude toward a favorable outcome.

After earning his degree in Holistic Health from the Ridman College for Complementary Alternative Medicine in Israel in 2000, Avinoam was certified by the National Guild of Hypnotists (NGH) as well as the National Federation of Neuro-Linguistic Programming (NLP) in the USA.

Much of Avinoam's work is founded on the work of Dr. Ernest Rossi as described in his breakthrough book The Psychobiology of Mind Body Healing and Dr. Al Barrios, a clinical psychologist and a pioneer in the field of immunotherapy.

Avinoam is also inspired by the work of Stephen C.Parkhill, a noted hypnotherapist and the author of *Answer Cancer – The Healing of A Nation*.

For more on information on

Holistic Cancer Care

Visit

AvinoamLerner.com

While there sign up for the

FREE WHITE PAPER on

Hypnotherapy for Cancer Care

You can also shop for Guided Imagery CDs

at AvinoamLerner.com/shop

or join our community and like our

Facebook page

www.facebook.com/HealingBeyondTherapy

References

Campbell-Gillies, Lynne (2005). The Effect of Guided Imagery and Relaxation on Patients Receiving Treatment for Non-metastatic Cancer.

Naparstek, Belleruth. Gifts of the Imagination: Surviving and Thriving Beyond Cancer

Davenport, Leslie (1996). Guided Imagery Gets Respect.

Dayton, Tian (2011). Reduce Anxiety and Depression with Guided Imagery.

Battino, Rubin (2007). Guided Imagery: Principles and Practice.

Naparstek, Belleruth (1999). Clinical:Case Study: Guided Imagery Part I: Use in Medical Practice.

Thomas, Valerie (2009). Using Mental Imagery and Visualisation Techniques with Cancer Patients.

PSYCHO-ONCOLOGY, Psycho-Oncology 14: 607–617 (2005). Published online 13 January 2005 in Wiley

InterScience   (www.interscience.wiley.com).   DOI: 10.1002/pon.889

22386542R00087

Made in the USA
San Bernardino, CA
04 July 2015